P9-CKZ-068

Stand Firm

Brinkmann, Svend,
Stand firm : resisting
the self-improvement cra
2017.
33305238809309
cu   04/28/17

nann

STAND FIRM

Resisting the Self-Improvement Craze

Translated by Tam McTurk

polity

First published in Danish as *Stå fast: et opgør med tidens udviklingstvang*,
© Gyldendal, 2014

This English edition © Polity Press, 2017

Polity Press
65 Bridge Street
Cambridge CB2 1UR, UK

Polity Press
350 Main Street
Malden, MA 02148, USA

All rights reserved. Except for the quotation of short passages for the purpose of criticism and review, no part of this publication may be reproduced, stored in a retrieval system or transmitted, in any form or by any means, electronic, mechanical, photocopying, recording or otherwise, without the prior permission of the publisher.

ISBN-13: 978-1-5095-1425-0
ISBN-13: 978-1-5095-1426-7(pb)

A catalogue record for this book is available from the British Library.

Typeset in 11 on 14 pt Sabon by
Servis Filmsetting Ltd, Stockport, Cheshire
Printed and bound in the UK by Clays Ltd, St Ives Plc

The publisher has used its best endeavours to ensure that the URLs for external websites referred to in this book are correct and active at the time of going to press. However, the publisher has no responsibility for the websites and can make no guarantee that a site will remain live or that the content is or will remain appropriate.

Every effort has been made to trace all copyright holders, but if any have been inadvertently overlooked the publisher will be pleased to include any necessary credits in any subsequent reprint or edition.

For further information on Polity, visit our website: politybooks.com

Contents

Acknowledgements

A vast array of books has been churned out on self-development, self-improvement and self-realisation. Millions of them are sold every year, and the philosophy of self-development is ubiquitous in the worlds of education and business. Our lives may be in a state of constant flux and change, but legions of coaches, therapists and lifestyle counsellors are on hand to steer us safely through these choppy waters. This book is an attempt to voice opposition – to posit an alternative – to the culture of self-development. In short, it isn't about how to develop, but about how to stand firm on your own ground. It's not about finding yourself, but about living with yourself. It recommends negative, not positive, thinking as your first port of call. It isn't inspired by pop philosophies like the Seven Good Habits, spirituality or Theory U, but by the sober (though never boring) philosophy of Stoicism, as formulated in Ancient Rome by both a slave (Epictetus) and an emperor (Marcus Aurelius). This may sound a bit strange at first ... but bear with me.

I would like to take this opportunity to thank

Acknowledgements

Lise Nestelsø and Anne Weinkouff for publishing the original Danish version of the book, even though it differs so starkly from many others in the Gyldendal Business catalogue. That is precisely why I thought you were the right publishers for the job, and I thank you for your trust and confidence in me. The whole process was enjoyable from start to finish. Anne was an extremely helpful sounding board, reader and editor. I would also like to thank Anders Petersen, Ester Holte Kofod and Rasmus Birk, who provided many valuable comments on the manuscript. Also, huge thanks to Todd May for positive feedback and for recommending the book to Polity Press – a publishing house under whose imprint I am immensely proud to appear. And last but not least, my thanks to Louise Knight, who was such an excellent and helpful editor during the production of the UK edition and to Tam McTurk for having provided a phenomenal translation.

Introduction:
Life in the Fast Lane

Many of us think that everything is moving faster and faster these days. The pace of life seems to be accelerating. We find ourselves under a constant barrage of new technology, rounds of restructuring at work, and fleeting trends in food, fashion and miracle cures. No sooner have you bought a smartphone than you have to upgrade to run the latest apps. Before you've even had time to get used to the IT system in your workplace, a new version is installed. Just as you figure out how to put up with an irritating colleague, the organisation is restructured and you find yourself having to get on with a whole new team. We work in 'learning organisations' in which the only constant is endless change, where the only thing we can be sure of is that what we learned yesterday will be obsolete tomorrow. Lifelong learning and skills enhancement have become key concepts throughout the education system, in business and in other sectors.

Sociologists use metaphors like 'liquid modernity' to describe our era, in which everything is in a state of perpetual change.[1] *Time* in particular is seen as liquid

– it's as if all limits have been expunged. Why this should be the case, nobody really knows. And nobody knows where we're heading, either. Some claim that globalisation – or more specifically, 'the threat posed by globalisation' – means that constant change is inevitable. Companies need to adapt to changing demands and specifications, so staff need to be flexible and responsive to change. For at least a couple of decades, job ads have been regurgitating the well-worn phrase 'We are looking for somebody who is flexible, adaptable and open to professional and personal development.' Standing still is the ultimate sin. If you stand still while everyone else is moving forwards, you fall behind. Doing so these days is tantamount to going backwards.

Under liquid modernity – also referred to as flexible capitalism, post-Fordism and the consumer society – rule number one is that you have to *keep up*.[2] But in a culture where the pace of everything is constantly accelerating, this becomes more and more difficult. The tempo at which we do everything – from changing jobs to writing essays to cooking meals – just keeps speeding up. For example, we now sleep half an hour less per night on average than in 1970, and up to two hours fewer than in the nineteenth century.[3] In almost every aspect of life, the pace has quickened. We now talk about fast food, speed-dating, power-naps and short-term therapy. Recently, I tested an app called Spritz. It only shows a single word at a time, but increases your reading speed from 250 to 500–600 words a minute. Suddenly you can read a novel in a couple of hours! But does this help you understand literature any better? Why has speed become an end in itself?

Critics of the pace of change point out that it leads

Introduction

to a general feeling of alienation from the activities in
which we are engaged, and to a constant sense that
we don't have enough time. Technological advances
should, in theory, free up time – allowing us to have a
kick-about with the kids, make pottery or discuss politics. But the opposite is in fact the case if the time that
we free up (e.g. from routine or assembly line tasks that
are now automated or outsourced to the Third World)
is spent on new projects and filling an already packed
diary. In our secular world, we no longer see eternal
paradise as a carrot at the end of the stick of life, but
try to cram as much as possible into our relatively short
time on the planet instead. This is, of course, a futile
endeavour, doomed to failure. It is tempting to interpret
the modern epidemics of depression and burnout as the
individual's response to the unbearable nature of constant acceleration. The decelerating individual – who
slows down instead of speeding up, and maybe even
stops completely – seems out of place in a culture characterised by manic development, and may be interpreted
pathologically (i.e. diagnosed as clinically depressed).[4]
   How do you keep up in an accelerating culture?
Keeping up implies a constant willingness to adapt. It
implies ongoing development on both a personal and
professional level. Sceptics refer to lifelong learning as
'learning until you die' (for many, interminable courses
by well-meaning consultants are a form of torture, even
a form of purgatory). In modern learning organisations
with flat management structures, delegated responsibilities, autonomous teams and diffuse or non-existent
boundaries between work and private life, it is our personal, social, emotional and learning competences that
are deemed the most important. In the absence of orders

3

issued by an authoritarian boss, you have to negotiate with others, work together and decide what feels right. Nowadays, the ideal employees are those who see themselves as reservoirs of competencies, and consider it their own responsibility to monitor, develop and optimise those skills.

All sorts of human interrelationships and practices related to what were considered personal matters in days of yore are now seen as tools and deployed by companies and organisations to drive staff development. Emotions and personal characteristics have been instrumentalised. If you can't stand the pace – if you are too slow, lack energy or break down altogether – the prescribed remedies are coaching, stress management, mindfulness and positive thinking. We are all advised to 'live in the moment', and it isn't difficult to lose your bearings and sense of time completely when everything is accelerating around you. Dwelling on the past is considered regressive, while the future is just a series of imagined and unconnected moments in time, rather than a clear and coherent life trajectory. But is it possible to plan for the long term when the world is so focused on the short term? Should you even try? Why bother when everything will inevitably change again? And yet, if you hold on to long-term ideals and stable objectives and values, you'll be seen as difficult and inflexible – an 'enemy of change', as the consultants would say. 'Think positive – and seek solutions' is the mantra, we don't want to hear any more whining or see any more sour faces. Critique is something to be quashed. It's a source of negativity – everyone knows that things work best when you just 'do what you do best', right?

Introduction

Mobility versus stability

Mobility trumps stability in an accelerating culture. You need to be fleet of foot, 'liquid', changeable, able to dance to multiple tunes and set off in any direction at any time. Stability and roots imply the opposite, that you're stuck in one place. You may be pliant, like the stalk of a flower, but uprooting and relocation are less simple. However, even in an accelerating culture, the term 'putting down roots' still has positive – albeit slightly olde-worlde – connotations. To have roots is to be connected to other people (family, friends, community), to ideals, to places, or perhaps a workplace to which you feel a certain sense of loyalty. Nowadays, these positive connotations are often undermined by a more negative definition of the term. Fewer and fewer of us put down roots in the demographic sense. We change jobs, partners and places of residence more often than did previous generations. We are inclined to talk about people being 'stuck' rather than 'putting down roots', and we don't mean it in any positive sense. 'You've grown into the job' isn't an unambiguously positive statement either.

Marketing is one arena is which these contemporary phenomena are particularly evident. Adverts are the poetry of capitalism – they are where society's subconscious, symbolic structures are revealed. A few years ago, I saw an ad for InterContinental hotels that read: 'You can't have a favorite place until you've seen them all.' The strap line was accompanied by a photo of a tropical island and the question 'Do you live an InterContinental life?' In other words, you can't feel *connected* to a particular place until you've been everywhere. This is very much the extreme end of the mobility-versus-roots philosophy. To tie ourselves down is to cut ourselves off from the other great places in the world. Applied to other aspects of life, the message is patently absurd, despite being relatively commonplace: you can't have a favourite *job* until you've tried them all. You can't have a favourite *spouse* until you've 'tested' all potential partners. Who knows whether a different job would help me develop more as a person? Who knows whether another partner would enrich my life more than the one I'm with at the moment? In the twenty-first century, in an age that prefers mobility to roots, people have profound difficulties in establishing stable relationships with others, including partners, spouses and friends. In most cases, their relationships with others are so-called *pure relationships*, i.e. based exclusively on emotions.[5] Pure relationships have no external criteria, and practical considerations (e.g. financial security) play no part. They are simply about the emotional effect of communing with the other person. If I am 'the best version of myself' when I'm with my partner, then the relationship is justified. Otherwise, it's not. We think of human relationships as temporary and replaceable. Other people are tools in our personal development rather than individuals in their own right.

This book is based on the premise that it has become difficult to put down roots, to achieve stability. All of us are now focused on mobility, on moving forwards. For the foreseeable future, there is probably little that can be done about this – not that it would be entirely desirable to return to a state in which our lives are governed by rigid parameters such as kin, class and gender anyway. There is something unique and humanising about liquid modernity's ability to liberate people from such strictures – albeit to a limited extent, because factors such as gender and class obviously continue to play a significant role in shaping the potential of the individual, even in modern, egalitarian welfare states. Many people, unfortunately, buy into the idea that they can 'do anything' (an idea foisted on the young in particular), so self-flagellation is a perfectly understandable reaction when their efforts prove inadequate. If you can do anything, then it must be your fault if success proves elusive in work or love (for Freud, '*lieben und arbeiten*' were the two most significant existential arenas). Little wonder, then, that nowadays so many hanker after a psychiatric diagnosis to explain away perceived personal inadequacies.[6] Another semi-poetic strap line – a slogan from the pharmaceutical giant GlaxoSmithKline, which makes products like the 'happy pill' Paxil – says: 'Do more, feel better, live longer'. These are the key goals in an accelerating culture, and psychoactive drugs help us achieve them: to *do more* (irrespective of what it might be?); *feel better* (no matter what triggered your emotions?); and *live longer* (irrespective of the quality of the extra years of life?). In an accelerating culture, we are supposed to do more, do it better and do it for longer, with scant regard for the content or the meaning of what we are doing. Self-development has become an end in itself. And everything revolves around the self. If we believe ourselves defenceless in a world that Zygmunt Bauman described as 'a global whirlwind', then we become more self-oriented – and therefore, unfortunately, all the more defenceless.[7] A vicious circle ensues. We turn inwards to master an uncertain world, which seems less and less certain as we become more and more isolated, finding ourselves with only our self-orientation for company.

Finding your feet

If mobility is the be-all-and-end-all of modern culture and it's difficult to put down roots, what *can* we do? At the risk of adding to the burden of expectations heaped on the individual in recent years, the message of this book is that we should learn to *stand firm* – and perhaps, in time, even find our feet. It's easier said than done though. The buzz all around us is about development, change, transformation, innovation, learning and other dynamic concepts that infuse the accelerating culture. Let it be said right from the outset that I am perfectly well aware that some people don't want to stand firm. They are doing just fine in the accelerating culture. While I do believe that, over time, they risk losing integrity and missing out on important aspects of life, I do, of course, accept their preference for perpetual motion. This book isn't for them. It is for those who do want to find their own feet but are unable to express this wish. They may even have tried to do so, only to be dubbed rigid, recalcitrant or reactionary by their peers.

Our secular age is shot through with fundamental existential uncertainty and angst, and this makes it difficult to stand firm. The upshot of this is that most of us are easy marks for all sorts of guidance, therapy, coaching, mindfulness, positive psychology and general self-development. In spheres like diet, health and exercise, a veritable religion has emerged that constantly churns out new edicts to follow and regimes to live by. One moment what you should eat is determined by your blood type, the next by the diet of your Palaeolithic ancestors. It seems that we – and I'm not afraid to count myself among the collective 'we' – lack purpose and direction, and run around looking for the latest recipe for happiness, progress and success. From a psychological perspective, this resembles a collective state of dependency. Carl Cederström and André Spicer call it the Wellness Syndrome.[8] Some (fewer and fewer) are addicted to cigarettes and alcohol, but a growing majority of people seem to be dependent on advice from lifestyle mentors, self-developers and health gurus. Multitudes of coaches, therapists, self-development experts and positivity consultants have emerged to help us change and transition in the accelerating culture. Countless self-help books and seven-step guides have been written to encourage and support personal development. Just look at the bestseller list – it always includes books about food and health, self-help books and celebrity biographies.

That's why I have written this book as a seven-step guide, in the hope it will turn on their heads some of the received ideas about positivity and development that proliferate in the accelerating culture. I hope you will recognise problematic aspects of the *Zeitgeist* from your own life, and perhaps build up a vocabulary with which to counter all the terminology of incessant development and change. The idea is that it will act as a kind of anti-self-help book, and inspire people to change the way they think about, and live, their own lives. I contend that in order to learn to survive in an accelerating culture – to *stand firm* – we should look to classical Stoic philosophy for inspiration, especially its emphases on self-control, peace of mind, dignity, sense of duty and reflection on the finite nature of life. These virtues engender a deeper sense of fulfilment than the superficial focus on permanent development and transformation. Stoicism is a fascinating tradition in its own right, of course, and one of the foundation stones of Western philosophy, but it is presented here for purely pragmatic reasons. Why reinvent the Stoic wheel? My interest is in Stoicism's relevance to *our* age and its challenges, rather than in whether I am interpreting it correctly in the context of its own time (probably not). My use of Stoicism is selective, and there are aspects of the philosophy to which I certainly do not subscribe (for a more detailed account, please refer to the appendix on Stoicism).

Stoicism originated in Ancient Greece and was later taken up by Roman thinkers. This book is not intended as an introduction to Stoic thought, e.g. as represented by the Romans Seneca, Epictetus, Marcus Aurelius and, to an extent, Cicero.[9] Rather, I use aspects of Stoicism to respond to some of the challenges of modern life:

- Where positive visualisation is preached nowadays (think of all the things you want to achieve!), the Stoics recommend negative visualisation (what would happen if you lost what you have?)
- Where you are now encouraged to think in terms of constant opportunities, the Stoics recommend that you acknowledge and rejoice in your limitations
- Where you are now expected to give free rein to your feelings at all times, the Stoics recommend that you learn self-discipline and sometimes suppress your feelings

Introduction

- Where death is now considered taboo, the Stoics recommend contemplating your own mortality on a daily basis, in order to nurture gratitude for the life you are living

In short, this book is for the reader who seeks a language with which to counter the development imperative in our accelerating culture. The various crises we encounter – ecological, economic or psychological – are very much the result of a blinkered philosophy of endless growth and general cultural acceleration. While Stoicism is no panacea, it can perhaps inspire people to find new ways to live their lives, based on standing firm – on accepting what you are and what you have, rather than constantly developing and adapting. This may sound like a definition of conservatism, but I would contend that, in a culture where everything else is accelerating, some form of conservatism may actually be the truly progressive approach. Those who stand firm are, paradoxically, those best equipped to cope with what the future brings. I am only too well aware that this book will not resolve the fundamental social and structural problems that demand collective solutions and political action. But perhaps it can help *individual* readers who – like myself – are uncomfortable with current trends in everything from education and work to the private sphere, which seem absurd and grotesque when viewed in the cold light of day. I am also fully aware that the book, paradoxically, is a symptom of the individualisation it seeks to challenge. Nevertheless, I hope that in highlighting this paradox (i.e. by aping the form of the seven-step guide) I will draw attention to the ills of the accelerating culture. The examples I present to support my arguments are designed to show up just how distorted and problematic conventional wisdom actually is.

The following seven chapters expand on the steps along the path to finding your feet and standing firm. The aim is to help the reader escape a state of dependency on development, adaptation, therapy and lifestyle gurus. Anybody who has ever attended a course in positive thinking may think the book paints an exaggeratedly gloomy picture of our age. It's a fair cop! This is precisely one of the points of the book – that complaints, criticism, melancholy and perhaps even outright gloom and pessimism can be helpful. There is also a certain undeniable pleasure in stepping outside of the accelerating culture and noticing that the glass you were told was half-full is, in fact, half-empty. You, dear reader, will find this out for yourself as you proceed through the seven steps. You will learn to observe, perhaps with a mild degree of smugness, how others are engaged in a frenzied dash around the hamster wheel, chasing the next signifier, trend or conquest – be it an increased market share or a more attractive partner. You will probably realise how much you have done this yourself, and that it is a somewhat immature way to spend your life. It is important that children and young people are able to develop and be flexible – let there be no doubt of that – but as adults we should be capable of standing firm.

The negativity recommended in the book has its own refreshing psychology. But it shouldn't, of course, degenerate into nihilistic pessimism that leads to resignation, ennui or actual depression. Rather, it should lead to you accepting your responsibilities and duties, your lot in life. As the Stoics knew, reflection on the brevity of life and its many inevitable problems leads to a sense of solidarity with others who are in the same boat – i.e. everyone else. Negativity will give you the time and opportunity to look at, and critique, the problematic aspects of life. It will help you grow used to concentrating on what is important in life: doing what is right, i.e. doing your duty.

In its original iteration, one of the steps in this seven-step guide was 'Never trust a seven-step guide'. I still think this is good advice, but I realised that it was a little too flimsy to form the basis for a whole chapter. The seven steps are now:

1. Cut out the navel-gazing
2. Focus on the negative in your life
3. Put on the No hat
4. Suppress your feelings
5. Sack your coach
6. Read a novel – not a self-help book or biography
7. Dwell on the past

Each chapter starts out with a recommendation, after which I explain and exemplify why it is right to act in this way. Where appropriate, I refer in brief to the inspiration provided by the Stoic philosophers, and show how their thinking can inoculate you against the ills of the accelerating culture. I also offer practical exercises to help you stand firm. The appendix delves a bit more deeply into Stoicism. It is primarily for the reader who wants to know more about this tradition and its relevance to the modern age.

Overall, the book should be read as a self-help book – albeit one designed to wean you off others of the genre – and as a cultural critique disguised as a seven-step guide. The idea is to discourage over-reliance on your inner self and encourage a more rounded world-view.

1

Cut out the navel-gazing

The more you gaze lovingly at your navel, the worse you will feel. Doctors call it the health paradox – the more help patients receive, the more they self-diagnose, the worse they feel. Most self-help gurus will urge you to base decisions on your gut feelings. Don't. It's not a good idea (especially after a vindaloo). Once a year is enough when it comes to self-analysis. Summer holidays are a good time for it. To compound matters, this kind of soul-searching is often seen as a tool for 'finding yourself'. This will almost always end in disappointment, with you slumped on the sofa, munching Maltesers.

Analysing and finding yourself are two of the most all-pervasive concepts in contemporary culture. Although not identical, they are interconnected. To find out who you *really* are – not just who you've been told you are by your parents, teachers and friends – you need to peel away layer upon layer of false consciousness and learn to listen to what your inner self has to say. If you've ever had doubts about anything (and who hasn't?), you've probably turned to somebody else for advice and asked: 'What do *you* think I should do?' And the chances are that you were told to follow your gut feeling. We've been telling each other this for decades – at least since the blossoming of youth culture in the 1960s, when social norms and external authorities were cast aside in favour of personal soul-searching. Step One in this guide is to accept that you won't find answers by looking inside yourself. There is simply no point in attaching so much importance to gut feelings and introspection.

At first, you may think that this sounds counterintuitive, but actually it's just common sense. If somebody is in trouble and needs help, there's no point basing your reaction on how helping them would make *you* feel. What you need to think about is the other person. You need to base your reaction on the idea that it's important to help others *per se* whenever possible – regardless of how it makes *you* feel. Whenever aficionados of science, art or philosophy insist that knowledge of Einstein, Mozart or Wittgenstein enriches the human experience, you don't ask yourself 'Yes, but how does it make me feel?' before deciding whether they are of any interest to you. What you need to do is take an interest in what these people actually *say*, rather than how their utterances make you feel. You need to learn to look outwards, not inwards; to be open to other people, cultures and nature. You need to accept that the self does not hold the key to how to live your life. The self is merely an idea, a construct, a by-product of cultural history. As such, it is by its very nature more external than internal.

This turning inwards to the self that emerged from the anti-authoritarian spirit of the 1960s has subsequently been institutionalised in schools and workplaces in many countries. School students are expected to find answers not just in textbooks or in nature, but inside themselves as well. They are expected to classify themselves as visual, aural, tactile or active learners, and tailor their personal development accordingly. Psychological journeys of self-discovery and introspection are lauded as means of learning more effectively. Employers send us on personal development courses, and managers coach us to identify and explore our inner selves and our core competencies. 'The manual is inside you', says the slogan for Otto Scharmer's mystical Theory U (to which I will return later). But perhaps the time has come to ask whether four decades of navel-gazing have really done us much good. Have we found ourselves? Is it even possible? Is it worth even bothering to try? My answer to all of these questions would be no.

Gut feelings

It has become commonplace to say we make decisions based on our gut feelings. Even senior executives in big multinationals readily spout the phrase. In 2014, an article in *The Telegraph* announced that 'the gut feeling is still king in business decisions'. According to a survey, only 10 per cent of executives said that if the available data contradicted their intuition, they would follow the data rather than their gut. The remainder would either reanalyse the data, ignore it or collate more information.[1] Some of them might even consult magazines or self-help books to find out how to identify their gut feelings.[2] The made-up guide below is typical of the advice given in lifestyle magazines:

1. Find a comfortable position. Close your eyes and turn your attention inwards. Take a deep breath, hold it for a moment and exhale. Repeat three times, then note the effect that the breathing exercise has had on your body.
2. Now become aware of your body, and relax it bit by bit. Start with the tip of your toes. As you relax, you will sense a more authentic form of contact with yourself, with your needs and your inner voice.
3. Observe what is going on inside you. When you start to feel something, don't try to change it in any way. Don't run away from it, even if it feels uncomfortable at first. This is where you make contact with your soul – or core, if you prefer.
4. Ask questions. All of the answers are already within you. So whenever you sense something you don't fully understand, ask yourself why. Ask yourself what you can learn from it, and trust that a response will be forthcoming. The answer may take the form of a thought, an image, a physical sensation or an intuitive realisation.
5. Use it. Begin to act on what you feel. Use your gut feelings to navigate through life. Once you dare to be open and vulnerable, you will start to grow. You will no longer have to adapt to the rest of the world. New opportunities will begin to open up.

This guide may well parody the frivolous end of the market, but the content isn't a million miles from what is recommended by all sorts of gurus and consultants in the mindfulness and personal-development industries. First you have to relax – something most of us would agree is nice once in a while. Next, it's time to 'feel your needs' by listening to your 'inner voice'. And this where it all starts to get a bit airy-fairy. Be on your guard whenever you encounter phrases like this. Is your inner voice actually worth listening to? What if it tells you the good-looking colleague beside you at the staff party is worth a snog, even though he or she has a partner? The authors of this type of guide would no doubt contend that at a staff party you aren't truly in contact with your inner *core*. Well, that's as may be. But how would you know? Only by delving ever deeper inside yourself, and ending up trapped in a vacuous circle that will ultimately leave you completely numb. Philip Cushman once posited that the depression epidemic in the West is explained by the fact that if you look inwards long enough – if you dwell on how you feel, and use therapy to find yourself – then depression will descend the moment you realise that there is, in fact, nothing there.[3] If, as is constantly asserted, the meaning of life is to be found inside you, then finding nothing there renders it all pointless. By spending inordinate amounts of time on navel-gazing you risk ending up disappointed.

You also run the risk of finding answers that are just plain wrong. The guide above says 'All of the answers are already within you.' Just think how absurd that actually is. What should we do about climate change? How do you make scones? What's the Chinese for 'horse'? Do I have what it takes to be a good engineer? To the best of my knowledge, the answers to these questions are not lurking somewhere within me or you – not even the answer to the last one. Society sets objective standards for what constitutes a good engineer (technical skills, mathematical understanding, etc.), and they have nothing to do with how you feel inside. These are abilities that other people are capable of assessing. The last step of the guide tells you to navigate by gut feeling: 'You will no longer have to adapt to the rest of the world.' As if! Only dictators enjoy the 'privilege' of not having to fit in. And it may ultimately may be more of a curse than a privilege. Emperor Nero – 'before whom a whole world bowed, who was perpetually surrounded by a countless host of the accommodating messengers of desire', as Kierkegaard put it[4] – had to set Rome ablaze just to encounter any resistance and to experience a reality that did more than just bow and scrape at his feet. Nero felt no compulsion to adapt to his surroundings. His whole world was but an expression of his needs and wants. However, we are human beings, not gods. People have to adapt to the world around them.

As mentioned at the start of this chapter, excessive self-analysis brings with it a genuine risk of feeling something that is actually meaningless, but that *assumes meaning* through the very process of feeling it. Since the 1980s, doctors have been referring to this as the health paradox.[5] More and better methods of diagnosis and treatment have led to people becoming trapped in a cycle of perpetual self-diagnosis, resulting in widespread discomfort and even hypochondria. In short: the more advanced medical science becomes, the sicker people think they are. Surely this alone is reason enough to cut down on all of the self-analysis? Something may well feel right, but to act on it instantly is to forget that it's perfectly possible you'll feel differently a moment or two later. The point is that gut feelings aren't sensible by nature. If you really feel like eating a biscuit but have a serious nut allergy, you'd end up cursing your gut feeling if you scoffed one with almonds in it.

Cut out the navel-gazing

Find yourself or learn to live with yourself?

The constant exhortations to think about how you feel are usually a precursor to 'finding yourself'. Pop psychology and contemporary culture propagate the notion that the real self – the ego, the core, or whatever you want to call it – lies within us, and that the processes of socialisation and the demands placed on us by other people create a manufactured self that must be overcome. In the 1960s and '70s, self-realisation emerged as the term for the process of stripping away this *faux* self, of listening to your inner voice, reflecting on how you feel inside and, therefore, being authentic.

You have already read above that the idea of the inner voice deserves to be treated with a dose of healthy scepticism. You might also ask why it is assumed that it is inside ourselves that we are most truly 'ourselves'. Why is the self not reflected in our actions, our lives and our relationships with others, i.e. in all that is external to us? The philosopher Slavoj Žižek put it like this:

> What interests me is [...] how there can be more truth in the mask that you adopt than in your real, inner self. I've always believed in masks, never in the emancipatory potential of this gesture, let's peel off the mask. [...] The true mask is my authentic, real self. And the truth comes out precisely in the guise of a fiction. [...] I believe in alienation, but alienation in the sense of [...] an external point of identification. The truth is out there.[6]

While psychology and philosophy have little to offer by way of explanation for the phenomenon of looking inwards to find yourself, sociology may offer a modicum of insight. Why did humankind begin thinking of itself this way? Why have we forgotten that the truth is out there, not inside us? The German sociologist and philosopher Axel Honneth provides one possible answer. He thinks that the idea that 'the answer is inside me' – and that the purpose of life is therefore self-realisation – may well have had a certain liberating appeal back in the 1960s.[7] At that time, there was no shortage of good reasons to throw off the shackles of a rigid society that placed unnecessary restrictions on personal and human development. Honneth argues, however, that while this inward turn may well once have constituted a legitimate form of resistance to 'the system' (patriarchy, capitalism, etc.), it has subsequently become the basis upon which the very same system now legitimises itself. He thinks that post-modern consumer society – which in this book I call accelerating culture – cultivates individuals who are flexible, changeable and constantly preoccupied with self-development and reinvention. To stand still in a society based on growth and consumption is akin to dissent. The self-realisation tsunami has aided and abetted the market's demand for a servile and flexible workforce, which is why, over the last fifty years, all sorts of ostensibly progressive management and organisational theories have focused on 'the whole person', 'human resources' and the idea of self-realisation through work.[8]

Self-realisation is no longer a liberating concept. Rather, it involves you accepting the idea of an inner self that you must develop, and perhaps even capitalise on, in ways that are designed to benefit your place of work. Nowadays, real resistance to the system consists not of turning inwards in search of some self or other,

Cut out the navel-gazing

but in rejecting the whole concept and finding out how
to live with yourself. The sentence 'I don't need to
develop myself' is rarely uttered during performance
and development reviews – indeed, given the prevailing
orthodoxy, it would be tantamount to heresy.

The paradox machine

The paradox of resistance to the system taking the
form of just standing still is perhaps best explained by
describing culture as a paradox machine. By its very
nature, the accelerating culture quite simply spews out
paradoxes – particularly in the context of this whole
notion of finding yourself. It is a paradox if the very act
of striving for something specific actually prevents you
from achieving it. If helping people makes them dependent and in need of more help, then we have a paradox.
For some psychopathologies, this paradoxical logic
is built-in: trying to live a healthy life can become an
obsession, an unhealthy one. An ambition to categorise
the world into rational systems can become an irrational
obsession, etc.

As a society, we see the paradox machine at work on
a bigger scale and in all sorts of contexts: for example,
attempts to liberate the working class and its progeny
by deploying critical and anti-authoritarian 'learning-
by-doing' have merely reproduced inequality (and even
exacerbated it in recent years), as these children have
found themselves unable to navigate diffuse educational
structures with their myriad demands for autonomy and
self-development. The offspring of the middle and upper
classes have encountered no such problems. Similarly,

the humanisation of the workplace – as well as the introduction of self-management by groups, the delegation of responsibility and personal development via work – has led to what the sociologist Richard Sennett dubbed 'corrosion of character' (the individual no longer has a firm foundation on which to stand), to an epidemic of stress and to a dehumanising breakdown in interpersonal loyalty and solidarity.[9] In the accelerating culture, constant demands to be innovative, creative and constantly go that one step further merely serve to cement the existing (lack of) order. Reading contemporary management handbooks on using 'values' to work with 'whole people' who need to 'develop themselves' is like reading a '70s critique of capitalism. In short: the idea of transforming society by breaking down oppressive traditions and liberating yourself is now ingrained in society's oppressive reproduction of itself. Soul-searching as a means of self-development or even self-realisation has become the key psychological driving force in the accelerating culture and all the problems it generates. So, not only will it make your own life better if you drop all this malarkey, society will benefit too.

The act of acknowledging the paradoxical nature of our time may have a crippling effect on the individual, but it can perhaps lead to reorientation as well. The consequences are inherently paradoxical: conservatism and its penchant for tradition emerges as the true progress. Might what was previously deemed oppressive perhaps actually be liberating? Might habit and routine have greater potential than endless invocations of innovation? Perhaps he who dares be like everybody else is the true individualist? Like in Monty Python's *Life of Brian*, where the main character, who has been proclaimed the

Messiah, addresses his followers with the words 'Look. You've got it all wrong. You don't need to follow me. You don't need to follow anybody! You've got to think for yourselves. You're all individuals!' The Messiah lectures the masses on the need to be themselves and not follow him blindly. They must do what *they* think is right. To which the crowd responds as one voice: 'Yes, we're all individuals', apart from Dennis, who says 'I'm not.' Paradoxically, he confirms his status as a loner by denying it. Maybe it's the same with finding yourself: they who deny that it makes sense to attempt to find yourself may just be the ones who are most themselves – or at least have some kind of sense of self. Those who reject the whole find-and-develop-yourself ideology have more chance of living a life with a certain degree of integrity – with joined-up and enduring identities – and sticking to what is important in their lives.

Since Rousseau in the eighteenth century, we have believed that the key is to be yourself and listen to the 'inner voice', about which Rousseau was one of the first to write. His famous autobiography, *Confessions*, starts with the words:

> I have entered upon a performance which is without example, whose accomplishment will have no imitator. I mean to present my fellow-mortals with a man in all the integrity of nature; and this man shall be myself. I know my heart, and have studied mankind; I am not made like any one I have been acquainted with, perhaps like no one in existence; if not better, I at least claim originality ...[10]

He articulates the idea that being yourself has some kind of intrinsic value. No matter what you are like otherwise, just being yourself is valuable. This – you now know – is not the case. It is – without a shadow of doubt – better to be an inauthentic Mother Teresa than an authentic Anders Breivik. Indeed, being yourself has no intrinsic value whatsoever. On the other hand, what does have inherent value is fulfilling your obligations to the people with whom you are interconnected (i.e. doing your duty), and whether you 'are yourself' while doing so is essentially meaningless. Often, the quest to find the self will even lead to others being sacrificed along the way, making it impossible for you to fulfil your duties and obligations to others properly. I would argue that it is better to be in some doubt about what your gut feeling means – and about whether you have found yourself – than to follow your gut feeling and pursue the elusive self in a blinkered fashion. Once we accept that the self is impossible to pin down and gut feelings are unreliable, this very doubt becomes a virtue in itself. After Steps One and Two of this guide, Step Three provides a more in-depth introduction to doubt – including doubts about yourself – as a virtue. But more of that anon. First, you'll have to practise ignoring your intestines.

What can I do?

Given the above characterisation of the demands for navel-gazing and self-realisation that pervade modern culture, you would be justified in asking the obvious question: what can I do? Me, myself? How do you go about learning *not* to gaze expectantly at your bellybutton? The Stoic philosophers not only have answers, they even suggest specific exercises to help you out. Getting started isn't always easy but give it a go anyway. The most obvious suggestion is to do something you don't want to do. Something that doesn't feel right inside but might nevertheless *be* right for reasons that have nothing to do with how it makes you feel. The modern Stoic William Irvine calls it a 'program for voluntary discomfort'.[11] It doesn't have to be something dramatic, such as starving yourself for weeks like some latter-day ascetic mystic. In fact, it can be as simple as not eating dessert even though you want to and aren't on a diet. Or wearing clothes that aren't warm enough so you're a bit cold. Or taking the bus on a day when it would be easier to take the car. Or cycling in the rain rather than taking the bus.

'Is there method in this madness?' you might reasonably ask. According to the Stoics, there are multiple, interconnected, advantages to practising doing things that don't 'feel right inside'. Firstly, it helps us build up the strength to cope with whatever trials the future might hold. If comfort is all you know, and have ever known, it becomes extremely difficult to endure the discomfort that we inevitably encounter at some point in our lives, e.g. when we are sick and old, or when we lose someone close or something valuable. Secondly, it mitigates the fear of future misfortune if we practise discomfort on a minor scale. According to Irvine, enduring minor forms of discomfort teaches us that unpleasant experiences aren't necessarily something we should fear. Unknown futures are less frightening when you learn to cope with the concept that things won't always feel good when you delve into yourself in search of answers. Thirdly, we appreciate what we have when we've tried doing without. You like your bus pass so much more after cycling in the rain; your car after a long bus journey, etc. It's also a fact – and one that many of the ancient philosophers knew – that our appreciation of a meal increases significantly when we're hungry. If we learn *not* always to eat, even though delicious food is right in front of us, but to wait until we're hungry, the food will taste all the better for it. Give it a go: it's an easy exercise.

In Book 7 of his *Meditations*, the Roman emperor-philosopher Marcus Aurelius implored us to pay no heed to the 'agitations of the flesh'. Succumbing to 'the agitations of the flesh' is probably the Roman version of 'looking inside yourself' and following your gut feeling. He pleads with us to avoid it because otherwise we risk becoming slaves to our bodily urges. Such listening removes reason from the equation and makes it difficult to understand (and do) our duty in a given situation. The point is not to spend so much time thinking about what is inside you, and also that when the agitations of the flesh become so loud that it's impossible not to hear them, we must have the will-power to resist them whenever this is the appropriate response. Will-power is like muscle strength, the Stoics believed: the more we exercise it, the better and stronger it becomes. No matter how silly such innocent examples might sound, it isn't so stupid to practise turning down a dessert, a glass of wine or a lift in a car. Self-control is one of the absolutely key virtues for the Stoics, albeit one that encounters a degree of adversity in our accelerating culture, with its penchant for 'living in the moment' and its exhortations to 'Just Do It!' as the ad says. Put simply, we become better at insisting on what is important if

Cut out the navel-gazing

we learn to resist all sorts of – more or less random – incentives (either from the stomach or from whatever other source they might assault your senses).

The best advice I can give about practising *not* seeking answers inside yourself, and doing something that you don't feel like doing, isn't to throw yourself into all sorts of silly things, but to practise doing something that has ethical value. Even if it doesn't *feel* good (because acting ethically doesn't always). Apologising to someone who deserves it even if you feel a bit ashamed to be doing so. Or perhaps donating more to charity than you really want to. If the upshot, in the longer term, happens to be that this gives you a good feeling inside, so much the better. There's certainly nothing wrong with that, because now you know that it isn't a feeling inside of you that determines whether you are doing the right thing. A Stoic is, of course, allowed to feel good – including about their own actions. It isn't 'how-you-feel-about-it' that serves as the measure of whether you are doing the right thing.

Now that we've cleared that up, it is time to move on to the next step.

2

Focus on the negative in your life

It's much more fun to be a sourpuss than a happy-clappy type. And there are often plenty of good reasons for grumpiness, too. Everybody grows old, falls ill and, in the end, they die. If you spend time thinking about you own mortality every day, you'll appreciate life more. This is the Stoic aphorism memento mori – *remember that you will die.*

Once you've learned to tune out the constant psycho-babble and stopped making decisions based on gut feelings, you'll be ready for the next step. If you spend less time on introspection, you will probably have a lot more time and energy for other, more important things. But what to do with all this time? You already know that trying to 'find yourself' is a bad way to spend it. You run the risk of not liking what you find or of not finding anything at all. Maybe you could spend your time working on a 'vision' for the future instead? Or maybe you should try 'thinking outside the box' and imagining what life would be like if there were no limits on anything. After all, we are constantly hearing about the virtues of 'positive thinking'. Positive psychologists even think that you should foster 'positive illusions', i.e. think more highly of yourself than you deserve, in order to get further in life.

However, instead of focusing on all the positive things you have and would like to achieve, Step Two consists of learning to focus more on the negative aspects of your life. This has multiple advantages. First of all, it allows you to think and speak freely. A lot of people actually enjoy a good moan. Petrol's too dear, the weather's foul and OMG is that a grey hair? Complaining about anything and everything won't help you find the meaning of life, of course, but it *is* frustrating if you're not allowed to get things off your chest. Secondly, focusing on the negative is the first step in dealing with problems. There may be little you can do to improve the weather on Saturday afternoon, but if you aren't allowed to point out woeful conditions in the workplace – and you are only allowed to focus on success stories – then you'll end up frustrated and resentful. Thirdly, reflecting on all the negative things that might happen to you – and inevitably *will* happen to you (even positive psychologists die eventually) – will lead to greater appreciation of the life you are leading now. This is one of the main ideas in the Stoic philosophy of life, and the primary reason why the Stoics were interested in the ultimate negative: death. I'm not saying that they romanticised death, or thought it deserved to be celebrated. For the Stoics, death was something we ought to think about – but exclusively in the service of life.

The tyranny of the positive

The award-winning American professor of psychology Barbara Held has long criticised what she calls 'the tyranny of the positive'.[1] She thinks positivity is particularly widespread in the USA, but has become a kind of universally accepted international pocket psychology in most Western countries – we should all 'think positively', be 'resource-oriented' and see problems as interesting 'challenges'. This phenomenon has now reached the point where seriously ill people are expected to 'learn from their illness' and ideally emerge as a stronger person on the other side.[2] Countless self-help books and misery memoirs by people with both physical and mental illnesses talk about how glad they are that they went through a crisis because they learned so much from it. I think that a lot of people who have been seriously ill, or found themselves in some other kind of existential crisis, find it galling that they're expected to look on the bright side. Very few will say out loud that their illness has been awful from start to finish and that they would rather not have had to go through it. A typical book title might be *How I Survived Stress – And What It Taught Me*, but you're unlikely to find a book called *I'm Still Stressed – It's an Unending Nightmare*. Not only do we suffer stress or illness and eventually die, we're also supposed to think it's all so enlightening and rewarding.

If – like me – you think things are out of hand, then read on to learn how to eliminate the tyranny of the positive by accentuating the negative. It will make you better prepared to stand firm, where you are. We need to regain the right to think that things are bad – no holds barred. Fortunately, psychologists have started to wake up to this, including the critical psychologist Bruce Levine. Number one on his list of ways in which healthcare professionals add to the sum of human misery is the positive psychology mantra that victims should change their attitudes.[3] 'You just need to think positively!' is one of the most offensive things you can say to people in need. Incidentally, number ten on Levine's list is 'depoliticisation of human suffering', by which he means attributing all sorts of woes that befall people to their own personal inadequacies (lack of motivation, pessimistic outlook, etc.) rather than to external circumstances.

Positive psychology

As mentioned previously, Barbara Held is one of the sharpest critics of positive psychology, which has developed explosively as a field of research since the late 1990s. Positive psychology can be seen as a scientific reflection of the accelerating culture's fascination with positivity. It really took off in 1988, when Martin Seligman became president of the American Psychological Association. Seligman built his reputation on the theory of learned helplessness as a factor in depression. Learned helplessness is a state of apathy, or at least a lack of will to change painful experiences – even in situations where you actually have options that would allow you to avoid the pain. Seligman had developed the theory via experiments that involved administering electric shocks to dogs. When he (understandably) grew tired of torturing man's best friend, he decided to focus on something more life-affirming, and threw himself into positive psychology instead.

Positive psychology rejects the focus on human problems and suffering that previously epitomised much of psychology (Seligman sometimes calls standard psychology 'negative psychology'). Rather, it is a scientific study of what is good in life and human nature. In particular, it asks what happiness is and how it is achieved, and seeks to identify positive human personality traits.[4] As president of the American Psychological Association, Seligman used his office to promote positive psychology. He succeeded to such an extent that there are now study programmes, centres and scientific journals dedicated to the subject. Few – if any – concepts in psychology have so rapidly captured the imagination of the general public. It is thought-provoking that positive psychology has been so easily incorporated into the accelerating culture as an instrument for optimising life and all kinds of development.

It is, of course, perfectly legitimate to conduct research into factors that enhance well-being, provide 'optimal experiences' and improve performance levels. However, in the hands of consultants and coaches – or enthusiastic managers who have attended short courses in 'positive leadership' – positive psychology is rapidly reduced to a blunt tool used to stifle criticism. Some sociologists go so far as to talk about positivity fascism, which they identify in both positive thinking and appreciative inquiry.[5] The concept describes the kind of mind control that can arise if you only ever look on the bright side of life.

More anecdotally, I might add that, without a shadow of doubt, my most negative experiences in academia

Focus on the negative in your life

have involved positive psychologists. A couple of years ago, I was critical of positive psychology in a women's magazine and a newspaper. The reaction was dramatic.[6] Three positive psychologists, whose names I won't mention here, accused me of 'scientific dishonesty' and submitted a complaint against me to the senior management at my university. Accusations just don't come any more serious in the academic world. The gist of it was that I had presented positive psychology as unambiguously negative, and that I had deliberately conflated research into positive psychology with its practical application. Fortunately, the university flatly rejected the complaint, but I found the psychologists' reaction deeply concerning. Rather than writing a letter to the editor and discussing it in an open forum, the positive psychologists chose to malign my academic integrity to the management of my university. I mention the story because it is ironic that these positive psychologists were so reluctant to engage in open scientific discussion. Clearly, there are limits to openness and the appreciative approach. (I hasten to add that not all representatives of positive psychology are like that, thankfully.) Paradoxically, the incident confirmed my critique of the tyranny of the positive – it revealed that negativity and criticism (especially of positive psychology itself!) must be eliminated, and apparently by any means possible.

The positive, acknowledging, appreciative leader

If you have had any contact with positive psychology – e.g. in education or at work, and perhaps been asked to talk about successes as part of a performance and development review even though you'd rather discuss an annoying problem – you may have felt a form of discomfort that is hard to put into words. Who doesn't want to be appreciated as a resourceful, skilled individual, and want to continue to develop? Modern managers like to acknowledge and appreciate their staff. The example that follows shows the kind of phrases used by managers to describe good practice when they invite employees to performance and development reviews. The idea is to make staff understand the principle behind the review.

> The performance and development review is a forum in which we talk about opportunities. By reflecting on what we do, when we do it well, what makes collaboration in the workplace function as smoothly as possible and what maximises job satisfaction, we learn about the factors that drive development and what it takes to achieve our goals.
>
> My wish is that the performance and development review will identify what it is we do when things are going really well. I want to invite you to build on the successes in your working life.[7]

A modern manager doesn't want to be seen as a hard and fast authority, giving orders and deciding everything, but as someone who exerts a completely different kind of soft power by 'inviting' staff members to conversations about 'successes' in order to 'maximise job satisfaction'. Forget all about the fact that there is still a distinct asymmetry of power between management and staff, and that some goals are clearly more legitimate than others. For example, in my otherwise excellent workplace, we were recently asked to formulate 'visions' for how to develop it. My suggestion that we should strive to become a mediocre institute aroused little enthusiasm. I thought it was a realistic goal worth pursuing for a small university. But everything has to be 'world class' or 'in the top 5' nowadays – and this success invariably lies at the end of a road paved with opportunities and successes. I call this 'coercive positivity'. Only the best is good enough, and it is achieved simply by dreaming big and thinking positive.

Blaming the victim

According to critics of coercive positivity, including the aforementioned Barbara Held, one outcome of the unchallenged focus on positivity can be 'blaming the victim' – i.e. explaining away forms of human suffering or inadequacy with reference to the individual's alleged lack of a sufficiently optimistic and positive attitude to life, or a paucity of the 'positive illusions' advocated by positive psychologists (including Seligman). Positive illusions consist of an imagined self that is better than the reality. You think that you're a bit smarter, more competent or more effective than is really the case. Research suggests (although the results are not absolutely unambiguous) that people suffering from depression actually see themselves more realistically than people who are not suffering from depression. However, one fear is that the positive approach encourages a cultural requirement for positivity and happiness. In the accelerating culture, this paradoxically causes suffering, as people feel guilty about not feeling constantly happy and successful (see the paradox machine discussed earlier).

Another – but related – criticism concerns the playing down of the importance of context that characterises parts of the positive approach. If the hypothesis here is that an individual's happiness depends primarily on 'internal' not 'external' factors (e.g. various social factors associated with socioeconomic status, etc.), then it's your own fault if you're not happy. In his bestseller *Authentic Happiness*, Seligman concluded that only 8–15 per cent of the variance in happiness is due to external factors – e.g. whether you live in a democracy or a dictatorship, whether you are rich or poor, healthy or unhealthy, highly skilled or unskilled. According to Seligman, by far the most important source of happiness is 'inner circumstances', which are subject to 'self-control' (e.g. generating positive feelings, being grateful, forgiving, being optimistic and, not least, relying on the signature strengths that characterise the individual). Happiness lies in realising our inner strengths and nurturing positive emotions. This emphasis on the importance of 'the inner', of that which is under the control of our will-power, contributes to the problematic ideology that requires the individual to keep up and develop at all times – which includes developing the capacity to think positively in order to survive in the accelerating culture.

Kvetching

Barbara Held posits an alternative to coercive positivity – namely, complaining. She has even written a bestseller about how to moan and complain. It's a kind of self-help book for curmudgeons: *Stop Smiling, Start Kvetching*.[8] 'Kvetching' is a Yiddish word roughly equivalent to 'grumbling'. I might not be an expert in

Jewish culture (my main source of knowledge is Woody Allen's films), but I get the impression that a general acceptance of griping about things both big and small is actually a cultural conduit that fosters collective happiness and satisfaction. A good old public moan is a fine thing – it gives people something to talk about and fosters a certain sense of community.

The basic premise of Held's moaners' charter is that life is never completely okay. Sometimes it's just slightly less not-okay. This means that there is always something to complain about. When house prices fall, we complain about negative equity. When house prices rise, we complain about people constantly harping on about the value of their properties. Life is hard. But according to Held, this isn't our real problem. The real problem is that we are forced to pretend that life isn't hard. You're expected to say 'Fine!' when asked how you're doing. Even if your spouse has just had an affair. Improving your ability to focus on the negative – and complain about it – gives you a coping mechanism that makes life slightly more manageable. But complaining and dissent aren't just about coping with situations. The freedom to grumble comes from the ability to face reality and accept it as it is. It endows you with a type of human dignity, in stark contrast to the terminally positive individual, who zealously insists there's no such thing as bad weather (just inappropriate clothing). Well actually, Mr Happy, bad weather is real – and when it's bad, it's nice to be able to complain from the warmth of the pub.

We need to reserve the right to moan, even if it doesn't lead to positive changes. But if it *can* lead to positive changes then it is, of course, important. Usually, kvetching is directed outward. We moan about the weather, politicians or football teams. It's always about something else – not us! By contrast, the positive attitude is directed inwards – if something's wrong, we are required to work on ourselves and what motivates us. Everything is our own fault. Unemployed people aren't entitled to complain about the benefits system. They just need to get their act together, think positively and find a job. It's all about 'believing in yourself' – but that's a totally blinkered concept. It reduces important social, political and economic problems to a matter of individual motivation and positivity.

Getting on with life

My old gran is wont to tell people to 'get on with life'. When something is difficult, she doesn't think we should try to 'deal with it'. That's too much to ask. Dealing with something means mastering it, of course, or removing or abolishing the problem completely. But lots of things just can't be done away with like that. People are vulnerable and fragile, fall ill and eventually die. We can't just 'deal with' death in that sense of the phrase. But we can get on with life. In other words, accept problems but learn to live with them. This also provides an opportunity to stand firm. If something can't be changed, you might as well stand by it. Better to face reality than 'live in a fool's paradise', as my gran would say. 'Better to be Socrates dissatisfied, than a fool satisfied', as the British utilitarian John Stuart Mill said in the nineteenth century. Not everything is possible. Not everything turns into positive happiness. However, there are other aspects of life that are worth striving for, such as dignity and a sense of reality. The point is that you must dare to face up to negativity. You might be able to make some positive changes but, quite simply, the negative aspects of life are here to stay. Accept it. However, we must be allowed to complain and criticise. If we are blinkered, positive and optimistic all of the time, we run the risk of the shock being all the greater when things do go wrong for us. Focusing on the negative prepares you for future adversity. And complaining can also increase your awareness of the good things in life. 'I've got a sore toe – but the rest of my leg doesn't hurt!'

What can I do?

This brings us to one of the most important points in Stoic philosophy. If you want to be better at acknowledging the negative aspects of life, I recommend the Stoic technique called negative visualisation. As far as I know, positive thinking always recommends positive visualisation. You imagine something good happening to help make it happen. Athletes use this technique in their training. Their coaches help them to visualise their goals, in order to reach them. A typical book on improving self-esteem encourages the reader to indulge in positive daydreams. For example, 'enhance your self-esteem by imagining that you are coping in an admirable and fantastically rewarding way'.[9] As a counterbalance to such positive fantasies, you could take up constant complaining instead – but this would soon exasperate those around you, especially if you didn't do it with a twinkle in your eye. Stoicism's negative visualisation provides a more appropriate way of practising negativity.

Many different Stoics have worked with negative visualisation. In Seneca's letter to Marcia, who was still racked with grief three years after the death of her son, he writes that she must understand that everything in life is just 'on loan'. Fortune can take away whatever she wishes, without warning. This realisation provides all the more reason to love what we have in the short time we have it.[10] In another letter, Seneca warns that we shouldn't just think about death as something in the distant future. In principle, death can strike at any time:

> Let us always remember, therefore, that both we and all those we care about are mortal. [...] Because I didn't think that way, fate struck me suddenly, and I was unprepared. Now I think both that everything is mortal, and that this does not follow any particular law. Everything that can possibly happen at some point, can happen today.[11]

Epictetus recommends – directly and very specifically – that we think about our children's mortality every time we kiss them goodnight. This may seem over the top, but it demands that we consider the possibility that our child might not wake up the next morning.[12] It reminds us of our human mortality and, in doing so, strengthens our familial bonds and makes us better able to accept our children's mistakes. Most parents know the despair of a crying baby who won't fall asleep. But if we remind ourselves of the child's mortality, this despair can quickly turn into joy at his or her very existence. Epictetus would say that it is better to cradle a screaming baby in your arms than a lifeless one. The negative visualisation helps us to endure the screaming.

Ultimately, we need to consider our own mortality.

Focus on the negative in your life

Memento mori – remember you will die. Think about it every day. Not in a way that is paralysing or drives you to despair, but to help you gradually get used to the idea and appreciate life more. Socrates defined philosophy as the art of learning to die well. As mentioned previously, contemporary culture encourages us to focus on the positive. Everybody talks about 'the good life' – but not about learning to die well. Maybe we should. As the philosopher Montaigne wrote, 'he who has learned to die has unlearned to serve'.[13] The purpose of thinking about death is not to be fascinated by it for its own sake. Rather, it is through becoming accustomed to the idea of the ultimate negative that we avoid being consumed by the fear of death – and are therefore able to live better.

There are two aspects to negative visualisation, and here are two exercises to try:

- Think about losing something (or someone) you care for and note how this enhances the pleasure you derive from it/them. Psychologists speak of the concept of 'hedonic adaptation', i.e. that we very quickly get used to the good life. Negative visualisation can counteract hedonic adaptation and make you more grateful. Incidentally, hedonic adaptation is also studied by positive psychologists.
- Think about the fact that you will one day shed your mortal coil: Everybody grows old, falls ill and, in the end, dies. If you spend time thinking about this every day, then you will come to appreciate life more – including in times of crisis. Death isn't just something you can 'deal with', but with a little practice you might be able to 'get on with life'.

Stand Firm

Once you have learned to focus on the negative in life, we can proceed to the next step, which is all about learning to say no. It's time to put on your No hat!

3

Put on your No hat

Saying 'I don't want to do that' conveys strength and integrity. Only robots always say yes. For example, if you're at a performance and development review and your line manager wants you to take a 'personal development' course, just decline politely. Tell him you'd prefer to introduce a 'cake day' at work. Practise saying no to at least five things every day.

If you've completed the first two steps in this book, you will by now have learned to spend less time soul-searching and discovered the value of focusing on the negative in your life. That's not to say that you should never focus on the positive or engage in introspection. Of course not. The point is simply that you should reject the widespread misconception that 'the answer lies within you' and that you'll find it by 'looking inwards'. There is good reason to stand firm and resist the coercive positivity that permeates modern society, and tries to convince you that negativity is undesirable and dangerous.

Step Three is about becoming better at saying no. Over the last decade, we've heard all about 'wearing

45

the Yes hat', about appreciating, valuing and positivity. Well, the time has come to dust off the No hat and don it once again. Being able to say no signifies that you are a mature person with a certain degree of integrity. Learning to say no is an extremely important step in any child's development. While most parents (me included) want their offspring to be obedient to a certain extent, the first 'no' represents a crucial first step towards maturity and independence. As one child psychologist put it, 'the child now consciously enters into character as an individual and is capable of using language to distance itself from the parents. This act of opposition is the first step on the path to autonomy.'[1]

The idea of 'stepping into character' is important. Unlike popular psychology concepts such as personality and competencies (which you can 'work with' and 'develop'), the concept of character refers to shared moral values. The individual who insists on standing firm and supporting certain values based on their inherent worth – and is therefore capable of saying no when these values are threatened – has character. In this book, I use the word integrity almost synonymously. Integrity means that you don't just tag along with the latest trends. You live in accordance with a specific idea that is more important to you than everything else. Integrity means attempting to establish a coherent identity that transcends time and contexts – and standing by it. The opposite of integrity means always wearing the Yes hat, never doubting that saying yes is good and that trying something new is always a good idea. This type used to be known as a 'flibbertigibbet'. If saying no is crucial to independence, the good old flibbertigibbet, who never takes off the Yes hat, is the most dependent creature of all. If you only own a Yes hat, you risk falling victim to any old whim – personal or external. To use an old socio-psychological term, you are 'externally controlled' if you live according to the axiom that it's always good to say yes to whatever is on offer. In order to remedy this, greater internal control is required. Not that I am advocating a gut-feeling philosophy. Your gut feelings are just as likely to be externally controlled – because, in a communication-focused, networked society, they are affected by various influences (e.g. advertising). True internal control – called integrity in this book – consists of adhering to moral values, understanding the importance of obligations and duty, and using reason to determine what is good and right in a given situation. If you have integrity, you will often have to say no because so much of the accelerating culture deserves to be renounced.

So what is the Yes hat – and why do people wear it?

The term 'Yes hat' is usually something that we think other people *should* put on, but that they may be having trouble finding. In the workplace, you may be encouraged to don it if you are deemed not to be positive and development-oriented enough. The underlying premise is that it's good to say yes and bad to say no – which is, of course, absurd. Every single day we are faced with all sorts of temptations and inducements to which the answer should be no – and fortunately we often get the answer right. So why the Yes hat, and why is it justified? Perhaps we can find something approaching an answer by looking in greater depth at the positive 'yes culture'.

Nowadays, hordes of 'motivational speakers' clamour to help individuals and companies develop by saying yes. One example is Todd Henry, who on his website under the title 'Learning To Say Yes' writes:

> Unfortunately, 'no' can be more than just a word, it can also be a lifestyle. When our default posture toward anything unknown is to shrink back, hover around the perimeter, or generally opt-out, we are refusing the best of what life offers. [...] Creativity always begins with a yes. To create is to first say yes, then sort things out on the other side. It is to first say 'yes' to the risk, then to embrace it, then to overcome it. All creations are not successful, but every act of creating begins with an act of bravery. I've come to treat the very act of saying 'yes' as a successful outcome. If I do this enough times in a row, I know that I will eventually make something worthwhile.
>
> Are you living your life with a posture of yes?[2]

The excerpt above is peppered with positive words like 'creativity' and 'bravery', which the author associates with saying yes. The point behind calls to arms of this kind is usually that we should seek to find inspiration and motivation and be true to ourselves. In other words, we should focus on and work with the internal – in this context, primarily by daring to say yes. We do this by setting goals and being creative and courageous. You shouldn't do what others expect, but what you want to do. The paradox is, of course, that in recent years we have all been expected to set goals, fight to succeed and live 'as you please' – all while wearing the Yes hat. It is considered wrong to *not* want to be part of this network of interconnected demands. You might don the No hat too often – which is most definitely considered wrong (even if you 'want' to put it on).

Put on your No hat

It's not my intention to assert that Todd Henry and other Yes milliners are mistaken *per se*. In fact, they are on to something. But it's a problem if the Yes hat is deemed to be the only legitimate one. It's not that the Yes hat should be thrown away, but that we should have a range of hats. We should also have a No hat, a Maybe hat, a Doubt hat and a Hesitation hat. Firstly, it would be against human nature – as you learned in Step Two – to proscribe negativity and critique. Nobody can live up to that. Nor should they. To try it is to risk stress and depression. As we all know, people are different – some are sanguine, others are more melancholy. While the melancholic may allegedly be out of step with social demands for positivity and constant incitements to action, there is nothing wrong with a slight penchant for gloominess (it may even be beneficial, as it makes it easier to stand firm). Secondly, always having to say yes would reflect a rather servile image of humankind. Demanding that people say yes is degrading when it becomes a dogma that reduces people to servants who can be ordered to go anywhere, any time, and not put down roots.

But why is the Yes hat so much more *in* than the No hat? I think there are two main reasons. The first stems from the pace of the accelerating culture and the changing nature of what it has to offer us. When everything feels liquid and mobile (whether that is truly the case or not), the Yes hat is a way of making yourself 'good enough'. It emits the signal that you are sufficiently enterprising to keep up with what is going on. The philosopher Anders Fogh Jensen describes our era as 'the project society', one in which all sorts of activities and practices are conceived of as projects, and they are often fleeting, short-term and recyclable.[3] He describes how, as individuals in this project society, we 'over-book' ourselves with appointments and projects in an attempt to use our capacity fully – much like airlines do. Since our duties in life have become mere 'projects', they are, of course, temporary, and we just jettison them if something more interesting pops up on our radar. Nonetheless, the prevailing idea is that we should say yes to projects. The ability to squeeze out an enthusiastic 'Yes!' is a core competency in the accelerating culture, something to double underline in job applications. 'Saying yes to new challenges' is considered unequivo-cally good, while a polite 'no thanks' is interpreted as a lack of courage and an unwillingness to change.

The first reason why the Yes hat is far more popu-lar than its negative counterpart is the social fear of not being sufficiently enterprising or 'on the ball'. The second reason is more existential: it originates from the fear of missing out (sometimes abbreviated to FOMO). You put on the Yes hat not just to be attractive and 'employable' in the eyes of others, but also because life is finite, and you're supposed to think that it's impor-tant to 'make the most of it'. We need to see and do as much as possible in the shortest possible time – as the InterContinental ad quoted in the Introduction put it: 'You can't have a favorite place until you've seen them all.' If we don't put on the Yes hat and accept all of life's fascinating opportunities, we cut ourselves off from excitement, from adventure and from experiencing life to its fullest. Or do we? As you've probably guessed, this notion is the polar opposite of the Stoic ideals pro-pounded in this book. The Stoics see nothing wrong with positive experiences *per se*, but don't see pursuing as many of them as possible as an end in itself. In fact, such a pursuit, decked out in a Yes hat and the latest fashionable gear, might stop you achieving peace of mind, the virtue that the Stoics cherish most. An inability to say no – for example, because you are afraid of missing out on something – will throw you off course. It becomes difficult to step back and accept your current circumstances. But in the accelerating culture, peace of mind is no longer deemed a desirable state. It's a problem. People with peace of mind are precisely the type who are grounded enough to knock back all sorts of (unreasonable) requirements and demands. That is not an asset in an era when the ideal is the liquid, flexible, changeable individual.

The ethics of doubt in the risk society

Advocates of the Yes hat often accuse those who don the No hat of a lack of courage, and of rigidity and caution. But you could equally assert that it is the philosophy of the Yes hat that clings to certainty. I have already argued that the Yes hat became fashionable because we are driven by fear – of not being able to keep up, of missing out. To eliminate this fear (which is, of course, impossible) we must say yes. Generally speaking, proponents of the Yes hat are confident they know what's right. It is necessary, good and right to say yes, as it leads to positivity, development, etc. We *know* that saying yes is the correct path. Stoic philosophy asserts the opposite: we do *not* know whether it is right to say yes, and this makes doubt the preferable option. If in doubt, the answer is usually no, so you should always have the No hat at hand. In other words, 'if it ain't broke, don't fix it'. We know what we have now, but not what we will have in the future.

In one sense, the contemporary world lauds certainty as never before. Certainty is good – doubt is bad. The paradox is, of course, that of worshipping certainty while claiming everything constantly needs to develop and change. Maybe we worship certainty precisely because of the lack of it in our non-stop modern world? We come up with all sorts of ways to cleanse ourselves of doubt and achieve certainty in all sorts of contexts. This includes everything from political decisions (which are increasingly made on the basis of economic calculations rather than political ideas) to everyday life (where people insure themselves against more and more mishaps and pitfalls) and the professions (which have to be evidence-based – we want to *know* whether a teacher's practices produce the desired 'learning outcome'). Simultaneously, various ethical rules are drawn up to reduce doubt and make sure you are acting correctly. Doubt is considered hesitant, weak or uninformed. The doubter has stalled, and just needs to get a Yes hat.

Doubt and uncertainty have fallen out of favour, most likely because we live in what sociologists term a risk society, in which one of the by-products of development, especially in technology, is that new risks are constantly generated. Environmental, climate and financial crises are all by-products of this. One result is that the 'ethics of certainty' are lauded, according to which it is important to have certain knowledge. It doesn't really matter what the issue is – economics, health, education, psychology, etc. – science is deployed to establish this certainty. In the risk society, you have to be absolutely sure in order to be heard. You need to issue confident proclamations: 'Research shows that serotonin deficiency in the brain is the cause of depression'; 'We know that children learn in four different ways'; 'We now finally have a diagnostic system that deals with mental illness.'

Doubt is needed as an antidote to this. In essence, certainty is necessarily dogmatic, whereas doubt has an important ethical value. How do I figure that out? Well, certainty's 'I know' easily leads to blindness – especially when you know that it is best to say yes. Doubt, on the other hand, leads to openness, to other ways of acting and new understandings of the world. If I *know*, I don't need to listen. But if I'm in doubt, other people's perspectives are endowed with greater meaning. The problem with doubt is that, in the accelerating culture, it is slow and harks back. It doesn't lend itself to quick decision-making based on gut feelings and positivity.

From primary school to university, we learn to 'know'. But we also need to learn to doubt. We need to learn to hesitate. We need to learn to reconsider. The book *How to Stop Living and Start Worrying*, which consists of interviews with the philosopher Simon Critchley, turns self-help philosophy upside down. Normally you're told to 'stop worrying, start living and say yes!' But for Critchley, doubt, worry and hesitation are virtues. If all we ever do is say yes, we overlook the crises that stem from the Yes philosophy (Just Do It!), i.e. the constant acceleration of life and society. If we don't recognise these crises, says Critchley, 'human beings sink to the level of happy cattle, a sort of bovine contentment that is systematically confused with happiness (but maybe that's a little mean to cows)'.[4] As Critchley provocatively puts it, under the Yes hat lurks the laughing cow.

The ethics of doubt – the idea that we should doubt more and rejoice in the No hat more often – also includes a commitment to persistently doubting who you are yourself. Psychologists, therapists, coaches and astrologers compete to provide us with certainty about who we actually are. But perhaps this is an area where we would benefit from a little more doubt. The wise old Norwegian criminologist and sociologist Nils Christie puts it like this:

> Maybe we should strive to establish social systems with a maximum of doubt about who we are – and who others are. Recreate ourselves and others as mysteries. If psychiatrists are to play any role, it would be as communicators of the complexity of their patients. They should write short stories about the people they meet. In that way, perhaps lawyers and others might understand people and their actions a bit better.[5]

In Step Six, we will return to the role of literature, namely to how short stories and novels help reveal the complexities of existence in a markedly different way than self-help books and biographies.

So far you have learned the following: if in doubt, the answer is usually no. If you are not in doubt, try thinking whether you should be. As previously, the point is not that you should always say no, or always be in doubt, but that it if you are then it is an entirely legitimate state to be in. And more than that: more regular use of the No hat would be conducive to standing on your own feet and being true to the essential things in life. If you always say yes, you'll be put off whatever you are supposed to be doing whenever someone says 'Hey you, come here!'

At this point, you're probably wondering whether we aren't tying ourselves in contradictory knots in our attempt to develop an alternative to the accelerating culture's celebration of the rootless individual. How can you stand firm if you're also supposed to have doubts? What can you stand firm *on*, when doubt is elevated to the status of a virtue? The easy answer is, of course, to stand firm on doubt itself, i.e. to affirm the right to hesitate, the right to reconsider. This may sound like a trite answer, but in my opinion it is actually quite profound and has huge ethical value. Virtually all political outrages are committed by high-powered males, confident that they know the truth. 'We *know* there are weapons of mass destruction!'; 'We *know* Jews are inferior!'; 'We *know* that the dictatorship of the proletariat is a necessity!' When it comes to the important issues in politics, ethics and the art of living, it is human in itself to be hesitant and have doubts. *This* is actually worth standing firm on in a risk society, where the answers – and even sometimes the problems – are unknown. Another answer is that it maybe it *is* possible to stand firm on something about which you are also in doubt. The philosopher Richard Rorty proposed living this way as an existential ideal.[6] He described it as a kind of existential irony: that you recognise that the worldview you have is just one among many, and that at some point you will run out of justifications for it. But this doesn't mean you then just shop around for a different worldview. The ideal is to stand firm on what you have, and accept that other people may have different worldviews. This is called tolerance.

In her famous book about the human condition, the German philosopher Hannah Arendt expressed the ethics of doubt as follows: 'even if there is no truth, man can be truthful, and even if there is no reliable certainty, man can be reliable'.[7] Arendt wasn't a Stoic as such, but here, in the most beautiful manner, she expresses one of the tenets of the Stoic philosophy, and one that is particularly relevant in the accelerating culture of the twenty-first century: there may be no such thing as absolute truth, but that is exactly why it is up to us to create it in our own lives. There is no certainty in a rapidly changing world, but that is exactly why we have to be reliable, so we create islands of order and coherence in a world that is running amok. To create such islands requires that you are capable of saying no. In this sense, saying 'no' is a prerequisite for being able to stand firm.

What can I do?

Ideally, workplaces should have hat racks with equal numbers of both No and Yes hats. By that, I mean that it should be just as legitimate to point out why something *won't* work as to meekly acquiesce. Initiatives are regularly pushed ahead in the name of progress, often leading to a considerable waste of time and effort. Once you have finally upskilled to cope with the new systems and routines, restructuring comes along (again!). To allow the dust to settle, it should be standard organisational practice to reject a certain number of initiatives every month. Managers shouldn't just get all excited and present staff with 'new visions' to be given the nod. They should also pose the question: what unnecessary stuff can we cut out? The aim here is not just to practise lean management in the holy name of efficiency, but to focus on the essence of the work people do, so that researchers have time to conduct research, surgeons are able to operate, teachers have the chance to teach, and social and healthcare professionals are in a position to help people (rather than fritter away time on data input and evaluations).

If the No hat isn't introduced in your workplace (or if you don't have a job), start practising the difficult art of saying no on your own. At first, you may well get carried away and just blurt out 'No!' to any old request. Of course, that isn't the idea. Only say no with good reason. Maybe the suggestion is offensive, humiliating or degrading – or maybe you will just recognise that you have to stop overloading your life with 'projects'. Perhaps you are even starting to realise that other people (children, friends, colleagues) aren't 'projects', but human beings to whom you have commitments. As mentioned previously, it can't just be gut feeling that determines what you should say no to. So what should you base the decision on?

The Stoics recommend appealing to your own reason. There are things to which it actually makes sense to say no. It makes sense to say no to other projects until you've met all your prior commitments – no matter how exciting a new one might sound. It may be difficult because you don't want to miss out. In the preamble to this chapter, I recommend that you turn down at least five things every day. This is perhaps a bit steep, especially if the Yes hat has been welded in place for a long, long time. So try saying no to something you've long thought barking or unnecessary but kept doing anyway. For example, lots of workplaces insist on seemingly interminable meetings, which many of us fear – and with good cause. Try saying no to a meeting, and explain that you want to get on with your work. Say no with a smile. The goal of Stoicism is not to be a curmudgeonly naysayer (at best it is a means to an end), but to achieve greater peace of mind in the accelerating culture. If regularly saying no proves too much, try deploying doubt and hesitation to ensure that reflection and reconsideration are incorporated into your daily practice. Instead of immediately saying yes, try saying 'I'll have to think about that.'

4

Suppress your feelings

If you're always bubbly and positive, other people may suspect that your constant enthusiasm is a bit false. And if you're incapable of putting a lid on your anger, they'll treat you like an unruly child. Adults should choose dignity over authenticity. So practise keeping your emotions under control. For example, once a day, try to think of someone who has insulted or offended you – and send them a big beaming smile.

The first three steps in this book have taught you to spend less time exploring what's inside you, to focus more on the negative in your life and to wear the No hat more often. If you were to stop there, you might turn into some kind of cranky, irascible curmudgeon – maybe even the aggressive type who suffers road rage or is forever speaking ill of their colleagues. It's important that you read on, because you have to learn to harness your emotions – especially the negative ones – and sometimes you have to suppress them completely.

I want to be clear about what I mean by 'negative emotions' in this context. The fact that emotions like guilt, shame and anger are deemed negative doesn't mean they're bad or should be completely eliminated. These are all exceedingly human traits, after all. It simply means that they constitute responses to negative events in our lives. When something negative happens, it is good and desirable that our emotions are able to inform us about it. Contrary to what you will sometimes hear, it's vital that humans are able to feel guilt and shame. If we are incapable of guilt, we can't understand ourselves as moral agents with responsibility for our own actions, especially our misdeeds. Guilt tells us that we've done something wrong. Even if the emotion is negative, it's absolutely indispensable to living our lives fully. The same goes for shame. If we aren't capable of feeling ashamed, then we have no way of sensing how the world around us feels about what we say or do. Shame is a sign that you are acting in a manner considered unacceptable by your own community. You might even say that it would be difficult to become a mature, thinking being – with the character and integrity outlined in the previous chapter – if you know no shame. In terms of developmental psychology, this is described in Genesis, the Christian story of creation: Adam and Eve were basically animals, essentially naked apes, devoid of moral precepts. After eating from the tree of knowledge, they learned about good and evil, and began to feel ashamed of their nakedness. God gave them clothes and forced them to leave their paradisal – but basically animal – state. From then on, they became people. Humanity is inextricably linked with morality, which is introduced via shame. If the myth reflects any kind of psychological truth whatsoever, it is that being human is closely associated with the ability to feel shame. It is through shame that we see ourselves as others see us and assess who we

Suppress your feelings

really are. Without shame, we wouldn't be humans with a conscious ability to think for ourselves. In other words, we wouldn't possess the ability to relate to ourselves, which is a prerequisite for living a life based on reason.[1]

Since negative emotions are important, it is a worry if parents constantly try to shield their offspring from feelings of guilt and shame. These are the very emotions that lead the child into a moral universe, in which he or she will hopefully evolve, bit by bit, into a responsible stakeholder. When I was young, people would say to kids: 'You should be ashamed of yourself!' This is a phrase you seldom hear these days – and perhaps that's a pity. Ultimately, we need to acknowledge the importance of negative feelings. The same goes for positive emotions, of course, such as joy, pride and gratitude. But we must be careful not to put absolute faith in emotions, as is the current trend in some quarters. So-called futurists talk about 'the emotional society', while psychologists laud 'emotional intelligence'. A notion has been allowed to spread that in order to be *authentic* (which many see as the ideal) you must express your emotions when you experience them, regardless of whether they're positive or negative. If you're happy, then let rip with a song-and-dance routine. If you're angry, then for goodness' sake don't bottle it up. That would be inauthentic. Step Four teaches you to understand the problematic side of this cult of emotional authenticity, and to counteract it by suppressing your feelings. This will probably be at the expense of authenticity – but there are plenty of reasons to be sceptical about that concept anyway. Instead of trying to be authentic at any cost, a rational adult should strive for a degree of dignity, which assumes the ability to control your emotions.

The emotional culture

The accelerating culture is also an emotional culture. The sociologist Zygmunt Bauman – who, as previously mentioned, introduced the concept of 'liquid modernity' to characterise our own era – has mapped the evolution from a culture based on prohibition to one based on commands.[2] This trend encompasses a shift in outlook in relation to both emotions and morality. In a culture based on prohibition, morality consists of a set of rules that determine what you are not allowed to do or think. For instance, Freud's psychoanalysis was a clear reflection of a culture based on prohibition: society demanded that you suppress forbidden feelings, i.e. sexual drives, and sublimate them in accordance with established norms. If you were unable to do so, you developed neuroses, as a kind of psychopathological reaction to your excess of drives and emotions. Nowadays, however, neuroses are no longer the main psychopathological problem. The concept of neurosis doesn't even feature in the most recent diagnostic systems. Roughly speaking, neurosis was something that afflicted people in a society that demanded you put down roots, that required you to be stable and well-adjusted. If you failed to achieve these goals, neurosis lay just around the corner, like an off-the-peg pathology. Since then, mobility has replaced stability, and morals are no longer prohibition-based (you mustn't!) but command-based (you must!). Emotions were previously to be suppressed, but are now to be expressed.

The accelerating culture does not take issue with the fact that people are emotional, enterprising and grasping. The problem is no longer an excess of emotions, but the lack of them. I once heard a sex therapist say that people used to visit her clinic to talk about having too much libido, but now it's more likely to be about having too little. The problem today isn't the people who are (overly) flexible, it's the ones who are (overly) stable: they lack sufficient motivation, drive and craving to keep up with the ever-present demands for flexibility, adaptability and self-development. The category of mental disorder that denotes a lack of energy and an emotional emptiness is no longer neurosis, but depression. Nowadays, problems don't stem from emotions and urges, i.e. from wanting too much. Rather, there has been a shift in how 'too much' is quantified. And this continues to shift in a society that lauds development and change as virtues above all others. In an accelerating culture, there is no such thing as wanting too much. Instead, it is those who want more who win. One way of describing the issue now might be to call it the 'energy problem': I never get enough done! I don't have enough motivation, emotion and passion! Just look at the number of areas where the concept of 'passion' has crept in. A typical life coach, for example, will ask clients whether they live a sufficiently passionate life. By decoding the coach's words, we arrive at an accurate picture of the current command culture:

> You have to be passionate, you have to do what you love doing, it should be fun to go to work, you must make a difference – these are just some of the convictions that flourish in the world and the industry in which I move. And I'm so lucky because of that.[3]

In the accelerating culture, words like 'passionate', 'love' and 'fun' are increasingly associated with our working lives. This has led the sociologist Eva Illouz to describe the modern age as that of an 'emotional capitalism', in which economics and emotions are intertwined.[4] Emotional capitalism is a culture of emotions, in which feelings play a significant part in personal transactions between individuals. It is our emotional competencies that make us attractive in the markets (for both work and love). The concept of 'emotional work' is well described in sociological literature. It has long been particularly characteristic of the service sector, e.g. flight attendants who smile and are always cheerful to keep up the spirits of stressed and perhaps nervous passengers. Even while being abused, they respond in a positive and welcoming manner, which can be quite taxing for them. Some airlines even send flight attendants on acting courses, so that they know how to summon forth positive emotions.[5] These courses correspond to certain actors' penchant for 'method acting' – you don't just *play out* certain emotions, but actually *have* them. The keyword is authenticity. We want flight attendants who really *are* happy, not just pretending.

This kind of emotional work has now spread from the service industries to virtually every other sector. In organisations with flat management structures and plenty of teamwork, it's seen as crucial that you're able to be positive, co-operative and flexible in your human interrelationships. The core competencies are therefore personal, social and emotional. The same applies to the modern manager, who has to be equally passionate. Essentially, emotional life has been commercialised or commodified – we buy and sell emotions in the labour market. If we lack emotional competencies (or emotional *intelligence*, to use the psychological buzzword), then we run the risk of being sent on a personal development course to get in better touch with ourselves.

As you should know by now, too much introversion is a bad thing – it's part of the problem rather than part of the solution (to stick with the utterly bogus lingo of self-development). Instead of a self-development course, you could take an interest in the origins of the emotional culture. In his famous analysis from the late 1970s, the historian Richard Sennett wrote about 'the fall of public man'.[6] Public man lived in the old prohibition culture, in which his comings and goings in the public sphere were regulated by established rituals. He wore masks, rather than act authentically and play out his feelings in front of others. Sennett describes how this polite form of social convention gradually disappeared as the authenticity ideal gained ground – in particular, around the time of the countercultural movements of the 1960s. People began to be suspicious of established rituals (e.g. shaking hands), which they interpreted as suppressing spontaneous, creative and intimate contact between people. However, according to Sennett, they couldn't have been more wrong. He argues that societies have a need for rituals, as a precondition for people spending time together in civilised ways. There is nothing inauthentic about basing your behaviour in public on certain ritualised social conventions. According to Sennett, we suffer (literally) from the false idea that the impersonal and ritualised is morally wrong. He goes as far as to say that the modern age has produced a contempt for rituals, and that this makes us more culturally primitive than the simplest tribe of hunter-gatherers.

Modern society's pursuit of the authentic and emotional has given us what Sennett has dubbed the 'tyranny of intimacy', in which the ideal of human relations has become the emotionally based, authentic encounter (in private life, in education and at work). However, this ideal just leads to people constantly hurting each other. Could it be precisely this lack of ritualised social conventions that has led to the apparent epidemic of bullying in schools and workplaces? We have lost our sense of 'civility' or politeness, which Sennett defines as social conventions that protect people from each other but still let them enjoy each other's company. Wearing a mask is the essence of civility, Sennett writes in *The Fall of Public Man*. However, it is seen as inauthentic and basically morally depraved, whereas the opposite is the case (as Slavoj Žižek was quoted saying earlier in the book). Or at least this is the way it is seen in schools, workplaces, public offices, etc. In these contexts, a ritualised, polite mask may well actually be a condition for sensible coexistence. The growing emotional culture and therapisation of a range of social arenas is, from this perspective, deeply problematic, as we are increasingly invited to make our outward behaviour correspond with what we feel inside. On the whole, it is problematic – as we learned in Step One – to base choices on inner feelings. Perhaps we should learn from Leonard Cohen, who sings in 'That Don't Make It Junk': 'I know that I'm forgiven, but I don't know how I know. I don't trust my inner feelings. Inner feelings come and go.'

The consequences of the emotional culture

As Cohen says, there is nothing about feelings in themselves that means we must trust them – let alone express them. In an ever-changing cultural situation, our emotions probably also change faster than ever. One day we are passionately preoccupied by charity work, the next we're investing our emotions in the latest American TV series. At least, that's what I'm like – although I do try to avoid too much introversion. As a rule, our feelings don't constitute a foundation on which to stand firm. Rather, they change in response to prevailing circumstances and trends. It's an illusion to believe that delving deep into your inner feelings is the path to authenticity. There's nothing desirable about exploding in anger at a fellow motorist driving too slowly in the fast lane, even if it's authentic, even if you really *are* angry about it.

In essence, the worship of authenticity in the pursuit of true feelings infantilises us. The toddler who is swaddled in his feelings – who smiles when happy and cries when frustrated – is therefore implicitly presented as the ideal. Such children may be sweet and delightful, but this cult of the authentic and the childlike is highly problematic in adulthood. As an adult, you should instead admire those who are capable of controlling – even suppressing – negative emotions. You should also be careful not to casually hurl around positive emotions. When repeated too many times, 'Wow, that's megafantastic!' quickly loses meaning. Personally, I soon stop listening to people who've been trained in appreciative communication and gush with praise all the time. Put your emotions on hold until you really need them. If you 'hate' pâté, there are no words left to describe what you think of tyrants. And if you 'love' pâté, what words will you use to describe how you feel about your kids? The Stoic ideal of self-control may help you to put things in perspective.

Many will retort that it is completely wrong to suppress feelings. The consequences of doing so – especially of suppressing negative emotions – is that we end up burying our emotions deep inside us, where they fester and make us unwell. We have to express our feelings for the sake of our health! Do we really? The research into this is ambiguous. Suppressing and inhibiting emotions has long been associated with all sorts of ills – from low self-esteem to cancer. But the research findings point in many different directions. For example, some studies show that people with a tendency to suppress feelings such as anger run a greater risk of falling ill, and even contracting cancer – if they are women. For men, the opposite would appear to be the case. Men are more at risk of cancer if they give free rein to their anger.[7] Or, to put it in positive terms: the ability to suppress anger reduces the risk of dying of cancer – if you're male. However, I don't think you should put too much faith in findings like these, as the evidence is often open to interpretation, and, therefore, an insufficient basis for a philosophy of life. In their critique of the contemporary therapisation of life, psychiatrist Sally Satel and philosopher Christina Hoff Sommers summarised the research, suggesting that emotional restraint – and even outright suppression of feelings – can be healthy and conducive to a good life. They conclude that for most people, unbridled emotional openness would not help them achieve good mental health, and that it might instead be beneficial to put a lid on their emotions – even in the wake of tragedy and loss.[8]

Another objection is that suppressing emotions can damage self-esteem, because you learn that your emotions may be wrong. The obvious answer here is that *of course* emotions are wrong sometimes. If I react with frenzied anger because my toddler spills milk on the table, my emotions are not right! If I cheat at golf but still preen with pride at winning the tournament, my emotions are warped! I could go on and on. It is important to recognise that feelings are not always legitimate and should be controlled and suppressed. This is perhaps especially true of negative emotions like envy, anger and contempt – but of others, too. On top of that, it is also worth remembering that the whole discussion about self-esteem is often built on myths. In our emotional culture, we are constantly told that it's good to have high self-esteem and that low self-esteem is to blame for all sorts of ills. In fact, there is a great deal of evidence to suggest that the biggest social problems stem not from low but from high self-esteem, which is statistically associated with psychopathy and immorality.[9] In recent years, various studies have shown that high self-esteem is not quite the holy grail that those working in education and human resource development had hoped.

In brief, there is no reason to be afraid that suppressing negative emotions will damage your (or your children's) self-esteem. You may even pre-empt undesirable traits if you learn to suppress negative emotions like anger. Often, people tend to be angrier when they first learn to let rip. As an adult, you must master the art of emotional diversion – i.e. distracting yourself from your own anger, envy, etc., in order to reduce and even eventually suppress negative emotions. Psychological studies also suggest that if you put aside your negative emotions, you will be less likely to remember the unpleasant episodes associated with them.[10] You may recall the unpleasant things in life – e.g. if someone has mortally offended you – not just because they were unpleasant experiences, but because you yourself reacted strongly to them. According to the Stoic mindset, suppressing anger will lead to greater peace of mind and fewer bad memories that are capable of knocking us off balance.

But doesn't this imply a contradiction? Isn't suppressing negative emotions at odds with focusing on the negative, the importance of which was highlighted in Step Two? Well, yes and no. We're talking about two different pieces of advice for different contexts. Sometimes it's good to complain about negative things, and sometimes it's good to suppress anger at them. It goes without saying that neither of these responses is always unambiguously correct. Unlike ordinary self-help books, which have a tendency to recommend one specific solution (e.g. positive thinking), the message of this book is that reality is complex and there is never a simple answer. Never forget how important doubt is! And remember that being angry isn't the same as focusing on the negative. The goal for a Stoic is precisely the ability to focus on the negative *without* being angry – and either just accept it as an aspect of life, or try to bring about positive change if there's something you can actually do about it in practice.

What can I do?

So how do you learn to suppress your feelings more successfully? Take anger as an example. It was carefully studied by the Stoic thinkers, especially Seneca.[11] The basic idea is that anger is a key human emotion. Only adults can be angry – children and small animals can become aggressive or frustrated, but we rarely talk about 'the angry baby' or 'an angry cat'. The reason for this is that anger requires a reflective self-awareness not developed until adulthood and after we have acquired a sense of shame. Seneca defines anger as a revenge impulse. Although this impulse is very human, he emphasises that life is too short to waste on anger. You might want to see anger as a waste product of our self-consciousness, one that we need to tolerate, but also one that we seek to dispose of as soon as possible.

Humour is one of the key techniques for managing and defusing anger. According to Seneca, laughter is a helpful response to that at which we would otherwise be angry. For example, if someone insults us, humour is a far better response than aggression. Recently, the singer James Blunt was praised for having responded to various highly provocative comments on social media with very amusing responses that made the 'haters' seem extremely small-minded. To quote one of the more innocent from Twitter: in response to 'James Blunt just has an annoying face and a highly irritating voice', Blunt just wrote 'And no mortgage'. Try Googling Blunt's other responses to find inspiration for how to respond to insults that might otherwise trigger irate feelings of resentment. Seneca stresses that when you get angry (which isn't always avoidable), you should apologise for it. This repairs social relationships and may also strengthen the self. The act of apologising will often get you past whatever made you angry in the first place.

Epictetus recommended 'projective visualisation' as a technique to suppress anger. His example is one in which your slave smashes a cup and it makes you angry. (This is, of course, specific to Ancient Rome. If

71

you have a tendency to react with anger to the idea of slavery, you might wish to adjust this example to a different context.) Instead, imagine that it is your friend's slave who smashes a cup in their house. Were that the case, you'd probably consider your friend's anger totally unreasonable, and you would try to calm them down.[12] This allows you to recognise the insignificance of the situation and not fly into a rage. Marcus Aurelius was also preoccupied with the insignificance of things as an antidote to anger. In general, he recommends that you consider the impermanence of all things in order to avoid anger and frustration when those things disappear. If a cup is broken, it may well be a pity – especially if it was valuable – but from the perspective of eternity, where everything is ultimately doomed to perish, it is an extremely small and insignificant matter.

Life is far too short for anger. You must learn to repress emotions that disturb your peace of mind and prevent you standing firm. If you want to stand firm, it is a precondition that you aren't easily knocked off your stride. We are constantly bombarded with appeals to our emotions – on television, in social media and in advertising – and this constantly changes what we want. If you constantly pursue ephemeral desires, you can't stand firm. And if you can't stand firm, you aren't in a position to do your duty. You should therefore learn to suppress your feelings. This may be at the expense of authenticity – which is in itself a benefit. It bestows a certain degree of dignity on an individual to be in control of their emotions. Practise wearing masks. Practise not being affected by the pettiness of others. Once you've practised this, you'll be ready for the next step: firing your coach.

5

Sack your coach

Coaching and therapy have become ubiquitous development tools in our accelerating culture. A coach is supposed to help you find the answers within yourself and realise your full potential. But this is so wide of the mark. Consider sacking your coach and making friends with him or her instead. Perhaps buy the coach a ticket to a museum, and ask what lessons life has to offer if you direct your gaze outwards instead of inwards. Learn to enjoy what culture and nature have to offer – preferably along with your ex-coach. Go on a picnic or visit a museum at least once a month.

Of course, it may be that your coach or therapist has already resigned in frustration because you've stopped gazing quite so longingly at your own bellybutton and started focusing on the negative, wearing the No hat and suppressing your feelings. By this stage, if your coach hasn't already quit of his or her own accord, it's high time that you parted ways. Coaching promises that 'you will find the answers inside yourself', but you now know that this is an illusion. Coaching is perhaps the most visible manifestation of everything that's wrong with an

73

accelerating culture in which it is difficult to stand firm. The concept of coaching is based on constant development and change – regardless of direction and content. It is its own *raison d'être*. This is the case whether it is a service for sale, something managers offer their staff or something teachers offer their students.

In this step, when I call on you to sack your coach, I'm not necessarily referring to a coach in the literal sense – in fact, most people can't actually afford a coach (they often charge £100+ per hour). I'm referring to all kinds of representatives of what I call the 'coachification of life' (which could also be called therapification): the trend of surrounding ourselves with – and being dependent on – all sorts of self-development technology, most clearly embodied in the figure of the coach. The coach should therefore be considered representative of a wider trend in the accelerating culture. By preaching development, positivity and success, the coach is the counterpoint to the Stoics' praise for the peace of mind arrived at by standing still and standing firm. I use the term 'preaching' pointedly, because the coach is a bit like a high priest of our age, and has a quasi-religious obsession with the development and realisation of the self.

The coachification of life

Coaching has been a growth sector for many years. It has spread from the world of sport to education, business and life in general (in the guise of life coaching). In the accelerating culture, coaching is akin to a religion of the self.[1] In other words, coaching should be seen as part of a more all-encompassing worldview that revolves around the self and its development. Demand for personal development is seemingly insatiable. There's leadership coaching, employee coaching, teen coaching, family coaching, sex coaching, study coaching, spiritual coaching, baby coaching, life coaching, breastfeeding coaching, etc., etc., *ad nauseam*. Everybody wants to clamber aboard the coaching bandwagon. Coaching now informs related practices such as counselling, psychotherapy and pastoral care. A few years ago, huge numbers of my friends and acquaintances were training as coaches. There are now so many that few of those who completed the training have been able make a living as a coach. Nevertheless, the thinking that underpinned that wave of enthusiasm has spread to many areas of society.

Coaching has become a standardised way of stage-managing interpersonal relationships, especially when someone has identified a need for (self-)development. The coach drives us forwards – allegedly on our own terms and based on our own preferences. They are able to do so because they are not external authorities, dictating what is good and bad in our lives. According to the consumer mentality that epitomises our era, the customer is always right – so only I know what is good and bad for me. The coach's job is to help me learn about myself and my preferences, but not to dictate them to me. They must reflect my wishes and help me realise my goals. The coach asks questions, but the answers come from within me.

Coaching has become a key psychological tool in a culture that revolves around the self. As such, coaching is part of a more wide-ranging worldview that we might

– slightly provocatively – dub the religion of the self.[2] The religion of the self has taken over many of the functions of Christianity: the role of the priest is now played by a psychotherapist or coach; religious denominations have given way to therapy, coaching and other techniques for personal development; grace and salvation have been replaced by self-realisation, skills enhancement and lifelong learning. And finally, perhaps most importantly, where God used to be at the centre of the universe, now it is the self. Never before in history have we talked so much about the self and its characteristics (self-esteem, self-confidence, self-development, etc.). Never before have we had so many ways to measure, evaluate and develop the self – even though we basically have no idea what it is.

Unlike Christianity, the religion of the self does not have an external authority (God) to set the frameworks for life and human development. Instead, we have an inner authority (the self) that we now believe to be the guiding light of our lives. As mentioned previously, this is supposed to be why it is considered so crucially important to 'learn to know yourself', to 'work with yourself' and develop in the directions you want to. Upbringing, teaching, management, social work and many other social practices have therefore been therapised in recent years. The modern teacher is not an odious authoritarian conveying vast swathes of knowledge to a general audience, but a quasi-therapist or coach who personally facilitates the students' 'all-round personal development'. It's been a long time since teachers have used the cane, but today's teachers use 'psychological canes', e.g. different socio-educational or group-therapy games that facilitate social control through self-development.

These games are based on the idea that children's development is fostered by identifying their positive qualities in a highly individualised manner. The teacher may even have taken a coaching course that specifically addressed pedagogic issues. Similarly, modern managers are no longer remote authoritarians concerned solely with hiring, firing and administration, but listening, introspective therapists who, e.g. in performance and development reviews or coaching sessions, strive to develop the personal skills of their staff. When we go to work, the self goes with us – so we need to develop it in marketable directions. Above all else, it is imperative that we see ourselves as material for skills-enhancement projects.[3] In this context, coaching is a key tool with which to discover, rank and optimise our skills.

The dangers of coaching

The international guru Anthony Robbins, who has coached (and I kid you not) George Bush, Bill Clinton and Mikhail Gorbachev, says:

> To be happy, I think that there is one thing you need more than anything else, and that is progress. I have a key phrase in my coaching, I call 'Constant Never-ending Improvement'. I live by it myself. If your relationship is to be happy, it requires development. If you want to be happy with your body, it requires training. If your work or your business is to be successful, it requires progress.[4]

'Constant Never-ending Improvement' might be a useful slogan for successful athletes, but as a formula for happiness for ordinary people, it's a bit more dubious. The danger of coaching is, of course, that you will never be allowed to stand still. There's always room for improvement – and if you *don't* improve, it's your own fault. You clearly haven't made enough of an effort. The message is that everything is possible if you *believe* in it enough and *want* it enough. If things don't work out, it's because you haven't mobilised enough will and motivation. The consequence of this is that you automatically criticise yourself when something is problematic: you internalise external social critique and transform it into inner self-criticism.[5]

One problematic tendency in coaching is that if you're in a rut, exhausted, down, or running on empty, coaching is advocated as the panacea. The problem is, of course, that the exhaustion and emptiness may have been *caused* by the requirement for constant self-development and improvement. If this is the case, then further coaching risks amplifying the problems it purports to resolve. To put it bluntly, coaching is just more of the drug that made us sick in the first place! You may even find that you spend so long studying yourself that you realise there is nothing in there. At this point, the coach has nothing to work with, and the relationship becomes empty. Coaching basically revolves around somebody holding a mirror up in front of you to reflect your inner goals, values and preferences, and help you realise them. The very core of the religion of the self is the idea that the answers are to be found inside you. This both determines the direction of the development (where do I want to go?) and acts as a measuring stick for its success (when will I be good enough?). But given that this measuring stick is subjective, i.e. not bound by external standards, there is a risk of trying to develop in an endlessly expanding vacuum. When should I stop? 'Constant Never-ending Improvement' is the key phrase. You will *never* be good enough.

One of Anthony Robbins' many well-known inspirational statements is: 'Success is doing what you want, when you want, where you want, with whom you want, as much as you want.' The explicit message is that self-realisation defines the meaning of human existence – irrespective of the personal predilections that you pursue. Taken to the extreme, this way of thinking resembles psychopathy or antisocial personality disorder, because it encourages you to do whatever it takes to get whatever you want. Other people are, at best, instruments at your service, used to maximise your happiness and success. Success is doing 'what you want, with whom you want!' If we were to raise our children according to this definition of success, we'd just tell them whatever they want is good enough and that the point of education should be to teach them how to realise these desires. This is a clear example of the subjectivism that prevails in the accelerating culture and is encouraged by coaches via the religion of the self. In reality, bringing up a child involves teaching them about the boundaries society sets and within which we all must learn to live. The traditional concept of upbringing is based on the idea that there are things outside of the self that are worth knowing. It is generally accepted that it is the job of parents (but also nursery and school teachers) to bestow upon their wards the character and integrity discussed in the previous step, so that they recognise and remain within those social boundaries. But if you believe that everything comes from inside the self – ambitions, values, ideals – then the person bringing up the child is reduced to the status of a sounding board. In other words, to a coach, whose focus is on mirroring the internal rather than on defining values and boundaries.

The question is, of course, whether a parenting philosophy based on coaching principles – i.e. one that deliberately does not inculcate values or teach boundaries – could ever produce viable, properly functioning adults. Children raised in this way would probably become adults who focus on their inner impulses rather than understanding what is important in life and fulfilling their duties as human beings. They would be experts at looking inwards, capable of prioritising their own preferences and working out how best to realise them. But ultimately they would just be intelligent children. They would be experts in means-optimisation, but have no idea that they have duties in life that extend beyond their own individual and subjective perspective and preferences. In other words, they wouldn't realise that there are things that you should do because they're important, not because you want to do them (or not). There are aspects of life that are important, regardless of how individuals feel about them – but this idea is pooh-poohed in coaching and the religion of the self.

Coaching and friendship

For a lot of people, the confidence they have in their coach or therapist has virtually replaced traditional friendships. Man is an animal who not only mates – sometimes for life – but also *has* mates. Philosophers since Plato and Aristotle have recognised that friendship is fundamental to the human condition. According to Aristotle, a friend is a person with whom you spend time from which you both derive mutual pleasure. However, you also want the best for your friend for their own sake, and not just because you might benefit from them feeling good. A friendship is therefore a relationship that has its own intrinsic value: a friend is someone you help for the friend's sake. If you help others only to benefit yourself, then it is not strictly speaking a friendship, but a partnership based on an implicit contract (I'll scratch your back, you scratch mine). *Quid pro quo* (something for something) applies in many human relationships, e.g. between employer and employee, but not in the relationship between parents and children (where you have a duty to be there for the kids, regardless of whether you think that, as a parent, you 'get something out of it'). According to Aristotle, there is no *quid pro quo* between friends either. It is probably also safe to assume that humans are the only beings that have friends in this sense, since their relationships are based on give and take.

The question is whether the religion of the self, with its focus exclusively on the individual's preferences, and in which the coach provides tools for self-development, can be interpreted as a modern form of friendship. The answer is clearly no – the relationship between coach and client is the very epitome of an instrumental relationship. It is only maintained as long as the parties derive benefit from it and is often based on financial interest (coaching is a business after all). So there's something remarkable about the fact that the kind of dreams and secrets that, in the past, you would only have shared with your very closest friends have, in recent years, become part and parcel of coaching sessions aimed at realising the 'full potential' of the self. This seems to be one of the aspects of a more wide-ranging trend in the accelerating culture: that it is harder and harder to build proper friendships. The term 'friend' is already beginning to sound archaic (at least outside of the demeaning use of the term on Facebook), and there is a tendency to refer to 'networks' instead of circles of friends. But a network *is* instrumental. It is something you maintain, nurture and develop in order to mobilise it when needed. If you want to change jobs, you start by asking around in your network. Sociologists measure the range and strength of the network both qualitatively and quantitatively, as a form of 'social capital'. In this context, the concept of capital isn't really metaphorical. It signifies the commodification of personal relationships and the diminishment of real friendships. In the classical sense, as understood by Aristotle and the Stoics, friends are defined by their own value in a person's life – they are not just a resource to be utilised in the quest to get the most out of your own life. In other words, real friends are not something you buy.

What can I do?

If, like me, you feel uncomfortable with coachification and with the growing instrumentalisation of human interrelationships that it represents, then look at your use of language. Instead of having a network, you should talk about your circle of friends. In this context, the concept of a friend is very different to the way in which the term is often used, e.g. on Facebook. A

Facebook 'friend' can be just a contact, and nothing more. A network consists of relationships based on some form of contract. A true friend is someone for whom you want the best, someone you are willing to help even if you derive no benefit from the interaction. You can only hope that somebody considers you a true friend. In friendship, as in love, there are no binding contracts. So reintroduce the concepts of friendship and circles of friends, and sack your coach.

Who knows – maybe you'll end up being friends with him or her? Often, coaches are very good people, who have chosen their line of business precisely because they like people and want to help others. Together, maybe you and your new friend will discover that certain things have intrinsic value, and are not simply defined by their ability to maximise utility based on personal preferences – i.e. making the maximum number of our wishes come true. At this point, I would recommend two types of shared activity that might provide fertile soil for this budding new friendship: a cultural activity and a nature activity, represented by the museum and the forest. A museum is a collection of objects from the past (near or distant), e.g. art or artefacts that say something about a particular era or an aspect of the human experience. Obviously, you learn a lot from a museum visit – but the greatest joy lies in just revelling in the experience with no thought of how to apply the knowledge and information. In other words, the trick is to learn to appreciate things that can't be 'used' for some other function. A museum exhibits and celebrates items that, from one perspective, are little more than old (or new) junk. From a purely utilitarian perspective, this is, of course, irrational. But it reminds us that we stand on the shoulders of myriad intertwining cultural traditions from which our collective experience is derived. And might it not even be easier to stand firm when standing on the shoulders of others?

Similarly, a walk in the woods gives us a sense of being part of nature and an understanding that it shouldn't be seen as consisting of resources that exist merely to meet human needs and desires. The grass, the trees and the birds existed long before people, and will probably outlast us all. They aren't there for our sake. From a Stoic perspective, nature is a *cosmos*, which extends beyond the world of human experience. We shouldn't necessarily deify nature, but a little humility in the face of it can give rise to a healthy scepticism about the religion of the self (which emerges from a form of deification of the self). The easiest way to appreciate the intrinsic value of nature is to enter into it. Ask yourself whether the world would be a poorer place if the sperm whale was extinct. From the perspective of human utility, which reduces all meaning and value to mankind's subjective point of view, the answer is probably no. It is pretty immaterial whether the sperm whale dies out or not – it has no function for us. But most of us would probably feel a bit uncomfortable about this answer, and would intuitively argue that the world actually *would* be poorer without the sperm whale. This is the case even if we don't think we will ever see or interact with a whale. The same is true of museums and their collections. Who cares if some museum full of old rubbish burns down? The answer is plenty of us! Within the religion of the self – in which meaning and value emerge from subjectivity – it is difficult, if not impossible, to articulate a reason to worry about this. But the fact that many people clearly do care about sperm whales and museums highlights the warped nature of the thinking that underpins the religion of the self and the self-proclaimed wisdom of all these hordes of coaches.

Once you've sacked your coach and decided to reconnect with life beyond the self, the best thing to do is something that is good for another person. This might not be that difficult – so maybe it would be better to try to do something good for someone else without letting them know it was you. This isn't quite as easy, because it is completely at odds with the *quid pro quo* mentality. Anonymous benevolence will help you to understand the intrinsic value of good deeds. You will learn that it is not your own inner experience that determines whether something has value.[6] There are aspects of the world that are good, significant and meaningful in their own right – even though you derive nothing from them in return.

6

Read a novel – not a self-help book or biography

Biographies always top the bestseller lists, but often they just celebrate the trivial lives of celebrities and reinforce the idea that life is something we control. Self-help books do the same. Ultimately, they leave you despondent at your failure to realise their myriad promises of happiness, wealth and health. Novels, on the other hand, enable you to understand human life as complex and unmanageable. Read at least one a month.

Once you've sacked your coach, you'll probably suffer from self-development withdrawal symptoms. After being constantly preoccupied with yourself, your innards and your development, it's not easy to start concentrating on the world around you. Like an ex-smoker with a nicotine patch, you'll probably throw yourself into self-help books that promise to make life healthier and happier and lead you to self-realisation. Or maybe you'll do what most other people do, and read a biography. It's somewhat banal to say that the contemporary obsession with (auto)biographies reflects a culture of individualisation – but if that is the case, then it is only banal in the sense of 'blindingly obvious'. I also think

Read a novel

that there is something about the linear progression of the biography, in which events happen in chronological order, that has a reassuring effect in an accelerating culture that otherwise seems to be running amok. Both self-help books and autobiographies celebrate the self as the most important aspect of life – but it is rarely a self that is in any form of balance in terms of integrity and moral values. Instead, it is usually a self that is doomed to eternal development and change. Apart from this one, I've never come across a self-help book that seeks to help the reader stand firm and resist personal development. And you'll never see an autobiography titled *Self-Development: Its Part in My Standstill*.

Step Six seeks to break your dependence on this kind of literature of the self, which reinforces the idea that life is something it is possible to control – if only you know and develop yourself. Way back in the twentieth century, the philosopher Charles Taylor analysed how what he called the ethics of authenticity (i.e. that life is about being true to yourself) could result in new forms of dependence, in which people who are unsure of their identity need all sorts of self-help guides.[1] What causes uncertainty about identity and leads to a risk of dependency? Taylor says that it's because we have begun to worship the self in a way that seals us off from everything outside us: history, nature, society and anything else that originates from external sources. In the previous chapter, I called this the religion of the self. If we rule out the validity of external sources, we are left with only ourselves on which to base the definition of the self. This is at best trivial, and at worst makes it impossible to understand our duties and what is important in life.

Self-help literature is part of the problem, and should be ignored. However, since reading is generally a good thing, I recommend you throw yourself into a different type of literature instead – namely novels. Unlike self-help books and most autobiographies,[2] novels present life more faithfully – as complex, random, chaotic and multifaceted. Novels remind you how little control you have over your life, and also show how it is inextricably entangled with social, cultural and historical processes. Acknowledging this endows you with a humility that might help you to do your duty in life, rather than constantly honing in on yourself and your personal development.

The big literary genres of the day

Recently, the psychologist and sociologist Ole Jacob Madsen critiqued self-help literature from a cultural perspective.[3] His book analyses cognitive approaches (including NLP), mindfulness, self-management, self-esteem and self-control, and shows how these various methods of self-help fool people into thinking that, e.g. meditating or enhanced self-esteem will solve serious problems such as environmental and financial crises. Madsen sees a strong ideological imbalance behind most self-help literature, in which each individual is made responsible for their own destiny and must seek individual solutions to social problems. It is a fundamental paradox that self-help literature, on the one hand, celebrates the individual, their freedom of choice and their self-realisation, and on the other, helps create people who are increasingly addicted to self-help and therapeutic intervention(s). It is claimed that self-realisation results in self-sufficient adults, but it actually creates infantile, dependent adults who think that the truth lies within them.

Madsen begins his thoughtful analysis by citing Will Ferguson's satirical novel about the self-help industry, called simply *Happiness*. The main character is a sub-editor in a publishing house who happens upon a manuscript for a self-help book by an anonymous author. The book is published, and – unlike its competitors – turns out to be 100 per cent effective. It is an instant bestseller that cures people of their ills and makes them rich, successful and happy. The consequences of this all-pervasive epidemic of happiness are, of course, unforeseen and incalculable. All of the industries that feed off human misery (including the Mafia) turn on the publisher, often violently. The editor is forced to track down the author to save both of their lives. He turns out to be a cynical cancer patient, entirely free of illusions, who only wrote the book to guarantee some financial security for his grandchild. However, to counteract the destructive happiness epidemic, the author agrees to write an anti-self-help book – one perhaps not too dissimilar from the one you are reading right now.

This hilarious satire draws our attention to one incontestable fact: self-help books don't work! The reason thousands of self-help books are published – all promising to help us realise ourselves, develop and become 'the best version of ourselves' – is precisely because they have no particular effect. Or, to persist with the dependency metaphor, as the effects wear off faster and faster, an addict needs more and more drugs. The same is true of self-help literature – as soon as you begin living healthily, eating according to your blood type or practising 'mindful eating', you'll be tempted by something new and seemingly more exciting. There is always one more book to buy, one more concept to explore, one more course to attend. In this sense, the self-help industry reflects the accelerating culture's consumer mentality, as the products (including books) that promise to help readers find themselves are actually about endlessly changing the self instead – the 'Constant Never-ending Improvement' that Anthony Robbins preaches. Here we have yet another variant of what I earlier called the paradox machine. Overall, self-help literature promotes mobility rather than stability. You have to be yourself – and change all the time.

The same goes for the second biggest literary genre of the day: biographies. They constantly top the bestseller lists, because we want to read about how famous people go about realising themselves. Apparently, this is something achieved earlier and earlier in life, as the subjects of biographies are getting younger and younger. Any self-respecting sports star will have written an autobiography by the time they turn thirty. Many businesspeople, TV hosts, musicians and actors publish autobiographies, too – and the basic logic of the genre remains consistent. Life is presented as a journey in which the main character, by virtue of their individual choices and experiences, becomes their true self. A special subspecies of the biography is the type of misery memoir mentioned in Step Two. This is literature that describes a particularly traumatic experience (a crisis, divorce or mental breakdown) as a gift. Simply by thinking positively about your pain, it is transformed into a resource that gives you greater insight into yourself and ultimately improves your life. Autobiographies rarely describe crises that have exclusively negative outcomes. Far more often, crises and adversity are presented as opportunities for personal growth and development. And this may sometimes be the case. However, after reading this book, you also know that crises and adversity can also be just what they appear to be – horrible situations from which nothing good will ever come. More often than you might think, the best thing to do is to strive to live with dignity, by looking the negative in the eye and accepting it. But you won't learn that from typical self-help books or autobiographies (instead, look to Seneca and Marcus Aurelius for inspiration).

The novel as a technology of the self

On the other hand, I think that you can learn to accept adversity by reading novels. Novels are, of course, an extremely broad category, encompassing everything from potboilers to Russian existential classics. And, admittedly, countless novels follow the same linear templates that you'll find in self-development thinking. But the point is that the novel as a form is *also* free to showcase life and the self in all sorts of other ways. Our modern understanding of life as an autobiographical project is undoubtedly linked to the emergence of the modern novel as a literary form.[4] The novel – one of the first of which was Cervantes' *Don Quixote* in 1606 – portrays a particular individual's experience of the world, and explores how their perspective informs the world as portrayed in the book. This is in contrast to earlier literature, e.g. medieval canonical narratives in folk songs and stories, which portrayed 'everyone' by focusing on general situations that represented universal experience. The novel grew in parallel with the early stages of individualisation – as both a product of this development and as co-creator of it – and taught the reading public to understand the world from a subjective, first-person perspective.

As the genre evolved, the Russian literary theorist Bakhtin identified the polyphonic nature of the novel – in other words, the novelist is not limited to speaking with one voice, but is able to use multiple voices and even conflicting ones. Ultimately, however, we are still dealing with a single world, albeit one that is interpreted differently by the various characters. In recent years, new forms have emerged that are sometimes referred to as poly*theistic*.[5] The bestselling novelist and Nobel Prize nominee Haruki Murakami, from Japan, is an example of an author who has helped develop the polytheistic novel. This is fiction in which multiple gods (or worldviews) meet, where there isn't just a single world upon which many perspectives converge, but a multitude of different worlds that the reader is drawn into and pulled out of. The polytheistic element in Murakami is evident in many of his works, but perhaps most of all in his recent masterpiece *1Q84*, which features so-called 'little people' from a number of realities. In Murakami's novels, reality often changes shape. He could perhaps be considered a magical realist, though his work differs from – and is more melancholy than – that of the genre's Latin American pioneers, such as Gabriel García Márquez and Jorge Luis Borges.

In this sense, the novel has progressed from reflecting a single perspective on the world to multiple perspectives – and finally, to multiple perspectives on multiple worlds. Reading about Murakami's many worlds may make you feel as if you're on shaky ground. You start to doubt what you thought you knew – and if you remember anything from Step Three, it may be that our world desperately needs more doubters. We need an ethics of doubt, which is easy to say but difficult to practise. The novel is probably better placed to realise this ethic than philosophers and self-developers. I am convinced that the novels of Charles Dickens, Vladimir Nabokov and Cormac McCarthy (some of my favourites) will make us better people than Anthony Robbins' coaching guides or Martin Seligman's books about positive psychology. Admittedly, comparing fiction with self-help is like comparing apples with pears – but what they have in common is that they both explore what it is to be human and what life is all about. I wonder what would happen to our cultural perception of ourselves if we replaced Anthony Robbins' monotheistic worship of the self and its development with Murakami's complex polytheism?

As the novel has changed over the centuries, we have witnessed a development in those who read them as well. To use a term coined by the philosopher Michel Foucault, the novel is a type of technology of the self. For Foucault, the self is always interwoven with the technologies that shape and influence subjectivity. Technologies of the self is Foucault's term for all of the tools individuals deploy in relation to themselves, and with which they create, recreate and cultivate themselves as subjects (i.e. individuals who act) in particular ways.[6] Foucault takes various points in history and examines the technologies of the self that typify the age, e.g. Stoic letter writing, autobiographical confessions, examinations, asceticism and dream interpretation. It may appear as if Foucault's technologies of the self are equivalent to the concept of self-development. And in one sense, this is true. However, the significant difference is that while the self-developers of today typically posit the existence of an inner self to be discovered and realised, Foucault thought of the self as an illusion, something that is created, like an artist painting a portrait. It does not exist prior to its creation, and it does not come about by itself. Another difference is that the concept of self-technology is closely associated with an understanding of ethics. The concept of ethics plays an important role in Foucault's later work, as it represents the ongoing relation of the self to itself. Ethics does not, therefore, refer to an abstract philosophical discipline, but should be understood in relation to the subject's practical upbringing and education.[7] Being somebody, being a subject, consists not only of discovering and developing pre-existing properties of the self, but also of reflecting on the ethical dimension associated with being human. Further, ethics play a particularly significant role in a polytheistic world, where the aim isn't to find the truth about ourselves, but to live truthfully (as espoused by Hannah Arendt, cf. Step Three). The premise of this step is that novels will help you to understand these things better.

Literature without illusions

Fair enough, you might say, but *what* should I read? This is where it gets difficult. The answer, of course, will vary from person to person. In addition to stating the obvious – that the canonical literature from Homer, Dante and Shakespeare and numerous modern novelists is worth reading – I can only really recommend writers and books that have done me some good. There are insights in everything from Donald Duck to Cervantes, so I hope that my own favourites don't sound too elitist. I have already touched on Murakami, of whom I am a faithful reader, and whose vivid descriptions of everything from dreams to cooking put the reader in a meditative state that, in my opinion, far surpasses any mindfulness exercise. However, I will briefly discuss two other contemporary authors who have also been very important to me.

One is the French writer Michel Houellebecq, also a keen observer of the accelerating culture. He is famous, notorious and controversial. Some think he is a brilliant writer in a French positivist tradition that traces its roots back to Zola, while others see him as a sensationalist charlatan. I won't try to settle that controversy – maybe he's both. Nonetheless, his books try to show that our lives – and our ideas of the self – are the result of social and historical processes that are far too all-encompassing for any one individual to influence. His books also show (in an often humorous and satirical way) what is wrong with these social and historical processes. I have heard some people say that reading Houellebecq gets them down, but his work has the opposite effect on me. There is something highly edifying about his perspective – which is devoid of illusions – on our age and its problems.

It is difficult to determine whether Houellebecq's books are pure fiction, or whether they have significant autobiographical elements.[8] They constantly play with the contradictions between (biographical) fact and fiction, and between art and science. The protagonist is often reminiscent of the author himself, to the extent that in most of his books, the main male character is called Michel. In one of his best-known works, *Atomised*, the main character is raised by his grandmother after being abandoned by his parents, who were obsessed with self-development ('The couple quickly realised that the burden of caring for a child was incompatible with their ideal of personal freedom'). This parallels Houellebecq's own life.

A recurring theme in Houellebecq's work is the absolute commodification of human relations in the accelerating consumer society. In his novels, almost every relationship is characterised by an exchange of services, in which the individual's experience is their most precious asset – that against which everything in life is measured. Love is mostly described in purely sexual terms, and religion consists of nothing more than superficial and co(s)mic New Age philosophies, just another product in a marketplace of new experiences. Houellebecq's novels teach us that the pursuit of the self and self-realisation are basically reflections of late capitalist society, in which even the most intimate relationships are subject to commodification and instrumentalisation. Life is about experiencing as much as possible without finding external standards on which to stand firm, and therefore 'the destruction of moral values in the Sixties, Seventies, Eighties and Nineties was a logical, almost inevitable, process'.[9] Houellebecq's dystopian descriptions of key aspects of human life and the (dissolution of) identity in the post-modern

Read a novel

consumer society are at once precise and exaggerated.
In this sense, his books may be seen as a form of literary
sociology that analyses trends in the accelerating culture
and their human consequences. Something similar is true of the Norwegian writer
Karl Ove Knausgård, who has enjoyed huge international acclaim in recent years for his mammoth
autofictional work *My Struggle*. Over several thousand
pages, into which the reader is almost hypnotically
drawn, Knausgård reminds us of the fascinating details
of everyday life. Knausgård isn't as critical or satirical as
Houellebecq, but he is equally devoid of illusions – and
his books are even more closely intertwined with his
real life. But is his great work not an autobiography?
No. It is as much an autobiography as this book is a
self-help book. Or you could say that, by virtue of its
monstrosity, it deconstructs autobiography as a genre.
An autobiography relates the landmark decisions and
key events through which the writer has created or
realised him- or herself. Knausgård, on the other hand,
writes of seemingly trivial situations, e.g. about attending a politically correct Swedish children's birthday
party or his lack of sexual experience. But he doesn't
write about them in passing: rather, they are at the heart
of the book. It is not a self-portrait as much as a literary reflection on human life – on our relationships with
others, the family and nature. It may well be that neither
Houellebecq nor Knausgård's books are *correct* in the
objective sense (and both have been the subject of lawsuits, because they write about real places and people).
However, in a deeper sense, I think that their books
offer *true* descriptions of our lives, precisely because
they lack illusions and focus on negative aspects. They

97

don't present us with a grand Truth with a capital T (which, in any case, probably only exists for the religious among us), but offer true depictions of aspects of life in the accelerating culture. They show how stark, negative literature devoid of illusions doesn't have to be depressing and discouraging – on the contrary, it can be edifying, because it emphasises the importance of everything that lies outside of the self.

What can I do?

Read at least one novel a month. Most of us can manage that. I've already named a few recommendations, and tried to explain why writers like Murakami, Houellebecq and Knausgård are worth reading, as they offer an entirely different conception of the self than the one found in self-help books and biographies. We are influenced by what we read. If you choose biographies and self-help literature, you will be presented with the idea of the self as the inner and one true focal point for life. You are offered a positive and optimistic story of development in whose glory you are invited to bathe. Novelists offer a more complex, even polytheistic worldview. I'm not sure what would happen if we used these authors' works to interpret our lives, rather than self-help tomes. But I suspect that we would build up a more accurate picture of the world in which we live. They would provide polyphonic perspectives (Murakami) on social and historical processes (Houellebecq), and no detail from everyday life would be too small to escape attention (Knausgård).

How do novels teach us to stand firm? By helping us

find an external meaning or perspective on life upon which to do it. At least, that is the thesis of the book *All Things Shining* by the influential American philosophers Hubert Dreyfus and Sean Kelly. As the subtitle suggests, they want you to read the Western classics to find meaning in a secular age – a world without God.[10] Dreyfus and Kelly discuss writers like David Foster Wallace, Homer, Dante and Herman Melville, with a view towards encouraging openness to the world and what it has to offer – a skill they think modern humankind has lost. They contend that we are adept at introspection and preoccupied with our inner experiences, but have no concept of how to derive meaning from the world around us. They claim that the classics help address this shortcoming. Like Murakami, they call for a polyphonic and even polytheistic perspective, and find it in Melville, the multi-faceted symbolism of whom also encompasses the white whale as a polytheistic god (this sounds impenetrable, but read *Moby Dick* or Dreyfus and Kelly and all will be revealed). Unlike the monotheistic philosophy's distinction between external appearances and inner essence, as found in the religion of the self (and in the distinction between the internal, authentic core self and the outer mask), in polytheism there is no level of reality concealed behind the appearance. This could be a vastly influential idea in a culture like ours, which cultivates self-development. It brings to mind Oscar Wilde, who argued in *The Picture of Dorian Gray* that only shallow people do not judge on the basis of the external: 'The true mystery of the world is the visible, not the invisible.'[11] You often hear that our culture is superficial and only focuses on the exterior. If Dreyfus, Kelly and Wilde are right, the opposite is actually the case: we aren't superficial enough, and we think that reality is concealed from us. But under the surface, inside, there is nothing, no authenticity. At this point, having followed six of the book's seven steps, this should be abundantly clear.

7

Dwell on the past

If you think things are bad now, just remember that they can always get worse. And probably will. The past, on the other hand, has a tendency to become lighter and brighter, the further it fades into the distance. When someone presents plans for innovation and 'visions' for the future, tell them that everything was better in the old days. Explain to them that the idea of 'progress' is only a few hundred years old – and is, in fact, destructive. Practise repeating yourself. Look for role models who have put down roots. Insist on the right to stand still.

The accelerating culture is at one and the same time pre-occupied by *the moment* and *the future*, but is definitely not particularly bothered about *the past*. New Age and psychology techniques like meditation and mindfulness try to make us more present in the moment. In management and organisational development, Otto Scharmer's (he of Theory U infamy) concept of 'presencing' highlights the importance of paying attention to what is happening *right now*. But at the same time, the purpose of this heightened awareness of the present moment is to improve our effectiveness in a possible future. We have to be present *now* to succeed *tomorrow*. The business consultancy Ankerhus wrote about Scharmer and Theory U:

> We can't solve the fundamental problems of our age with solutions that belong to the past. We can't create new, innovative solutions to organisational and social problems by simply repeating the patterns of the past. Something new is needed so that we, individually and collectively, are able to move into a field where we experience our authentic self and learn to identify what keeps us stuck in outdated thinking and patterns of behaviour. It is this new social technology that Scharmer calls 'presencing'.
>
> On the journey through the U, we learn to face the future with an open mind, open heart and open will – and achieve our optimum future potential.[1]

Theory U is essentially the mindfulness concept applied to organisational innovation. Part of the message is that looking at the past means we only see outdated patterns that don't work today, and that it's only through being present in the moment that we experience our 'authentic self' (which you now know is a myth) and will realise our full potential in the future. The past is out – the moment is the new black. It is the key to optimising the future.

If you want to be a bit cheeky, ask adherents of the moment who is the most present in the here and now. The answer is, of course, non-human animals – they aren't burdened by the cognitive capacity to recall past events or transfer the acquired knowledge of previous generations to new ones. Non-human animals (but also babies) are present in the moment. What distinguishes humankind is surely our ability to transcend the connection to the present moment and, in a unique sense, draw on the past. Why has it become so unfashionable to look back at the past? Well, if this book's analysis is valid, this phenomenon is connected with the accelerating culture, which is, by definition, future-oriented and focused on constantly producing new ideas. There are even companies, institutions and consultants that specialise in 'future studies' – the idea being that it's crucial to spot trends in order to prepare for what lies ahead and help shape the future. In fact, futurists are more concerned with *creating* the future than researching it. They sell ideas and concepts (of the dream society, the leisure society, the emotional society and whatever else it has been called over the years) to their customers, who then adapt to what they have been told is just around the corner. This prediction then comes true precisely because they have prepared (and paid) for it. Once again, we find ourselves mired in a paradox: the way in which we prepare for the future shapes the future as a reflection of the way in which we prepared for it! If political scientists tell us that we need to reform our economy to compete with the Chinese in global markets, and we all accept this view, then that is exactly what will happen. When politicians say there's no alternative to the status quo – echoing Margaret Thatcher's famous TINA (There Is No Alternative) doctrine – then this becomes a self-fulfilling prophecy if the majority falls for it. The Thomas theorem, a sociological staple, says: 'If men define situations as real, they are real in their consequences.' This is how future studies – and indeed, our entire collective obsession with the future – works. Defining a specific trend as the real one means that it will have real consequences for (and in) the future.

This kind of thinking has led the philosopher Simon Critchley (whom we met earlier in the book) to conclude that our manic focus on the future and the eternal idea of progress is deeply damaging: 'we should as rigorously as possible divest ourselves of this ideology of the future and the cult of progress. The idea of progress is only a couple of hundred years old, and it's a really bad one. The sooner we're rid of it, the better', he argues.[2] We should replace progress with repetition and learn to dwell on the past. This is a more accurate expression of our humanity and reflects a mature attitude to life. But it's not easy. Children, teenagers and animals all look to the future (as they should), and human memory is far more forward-looking than retrospective. Memory provides a basis on which to act in new and unknown situations – it is not a tool for recalling the past for its own sake.[3] But recall is also characteristic of the human adult. We draw on the past and our experience to learn how to live our lives (to which I return below) and develop our culture. As Tom McCarthy says in response to Critchley's comment: 'We need to replace progress with repetition. That would be a much healthier world. Think of the Renaissance. Renaissance means rebirth. What they did was to say: "Look at these Greeks. It's great!" [...] And Shakespeare's plays: there's no claim to something new, he's rewriting Ovid or taking speeches straight out of the Roman parliament.' It is only in the past few centuries that we have started to perceive the new and future-oriented as having quality in itself. In fact, most things were better in the old days.

We have created a culture that draws up visions, makes plans and runs workshops about the future, and it is for precisely this reason that we forget our past insights and achievements far too easily. Concepts like innovation and creativity float around in all sorts of discourse about organisation and education, in which any sense of the value of repetition and the tried and tested has been lost. We are forever being told to 'think outside the box'. Fortunately, less excitable creativity researchers have pointed out that it only makes sense to think outside the box if you know that there *is* a box (and what it's made of). In most cases, it's probably wiser to balance on the edge of the box, only tinkering around the edges and improvising around tried-and-tested themes.[4] The new only makes sense within a horizon of something known. If you know nothing of the past and its traditions, it's impossible to create anything new that is useful.

The personal significance of the past

When we consider these issues in relation to our own lives, we find even more reason to focus less on the future and learn to dwell more on the past. To know and be able to dwell on your own past is a prerequisite for maintaining a relatively stable identity, and thus also for our moral relationships with others. If we want to live well in the moral sense, it's crucial that we know how to reflect on our own personal past. Mark Twain said that a clear conscience is the sure sign of a bad memory. Acknowledging your past mistakes – and dwelling on them without, of course, allowing them to fester and torment you – will help you to act properly. In addition to the moral teachings found in our history, it's also important for our self-understanding to think about our lives as something extending backwards into the past – it is there that we find the roots of our identity. In the novel *All the Pretty Horses*, Cormac McCarthy writes that the body's scars have the capacity to remind us that our past is real. It is an ancient practice among friends and lovers to study and compare scars, because they provide clear physical evidence of past events, and establish a link between then and now. Maybe we should introduce sessions during which people in organisations meet and compare scars, and learn to dwell on the past rather than formulating visions for the future?

In relation to this book's ambition of helping you to stand firm, dwelling on the past is perhaps the most important step. Knowing your past is a prerequisite for standing firm – because without the past, there is nothing to stand firm *on*. Several philosophers have argued this in recent years, including the aforementioned Charles Taylor, who thinks concentrating on the moment is only possible if you have a past to which you are able to relate. When called upon to answer questions like 'Who are you?' and 'What do you want?' (as we are constantly encouraged to do in the therapeutic development culture), it's better to provide an answer that articulates our lives and actions in a broader biographical perspective, than to pause and explore what we feel in the moment, as a kind of temporal snapshot. In order to know who we are, we must understand where we come from. The French philosopher Paul Ricoeur, in his seminal work *Oneself as Another*, tried to show that people can only be moral in the strict sense if they are able to relate to their lives as a whole, or as something that threads its way through time as a continuum and is best understood as a story, a coherent narrative.

Dwell on the past

He asks, rhetorically: 'How, indeed, could a subject of action give an ethical character to his or her own life taken as a whole if this life were not gathered together in some way, and how could this occur if not, precisely, in the form of a narrative?'[5]

Why is 'life as a whole' a prerequisite for morality or ethics (which in this context are synonymous)? Because, Ricoeur argues, if others can't be sure I will be the same tomorrow as I am today and was yesterday, then they have no reason to trust me or that I will do what I promise and otherwise live up to my obligations. And if I don't know my own past, if I don't try my best to establish a link between yesterday, today and tomorrow, then others have no reason to trust me. If I don't have what Ricoeur calls 'self-constancy', then neither I nor others will be able to count on me. Self-constancy – personal integrity or identity – is a basic precondition for trust between people – and hence for ethical life. We can only make promises and commit to actions together over time because we understand ourselves as being the same over time – because we have a more or less coherent identity. And we only have this because we are able to view our lives as a single narrative – as a story that stretches from birth to death. We must therefore learn to strive for self-constancy that refers to the past, rather than self-development that refers to the future. Many of us know people who have suddenly 'found themselves' and broken ties with family and friends, only to realise themselves in new contexts or on the other side of the world. A sudden shift in the course of your life can, of course, be legitimate (if, for example, you finally break out of an abusive relationship). However, if the motivation for this consists only of 'self-realisation', then this is perhaps a morally questionable course. If the self is to be found in our binding relationships to other people and the morally significant issues that characterise them – i.e. if it is *not* an internal thing to be realised – then true self-realisation is a consequence of ethical interactions with others.

Perhaps the argument can even be honed down to such an extent that only individuals with self-constancy feel guilt and are capable of being moral (apropos Mark Twain on a clear conscience as the sure sign of a bad memory). There is an intrinsic connection between the sense of guilt and the concept of the promise – both are fundamental human phenomena. If we didn't have the ability to make promises, then marriages or other long-term relationships based on fidelity (perhaps even 'till death do us part') would be impossible. Nor would it be possible to enter into agreements and contracts for goods or property ('I promise to pay tomorrow'). Day-to-day life couldn't function either, as it is based on the constant making of promises ('I'll do the dishes') – both big and small, explicit and implicit. No human community or society would be sustainable without our fundamental ability to make and keep promises. To make a promise is to declare yourself willing to be held accountable for ensuring that what you say you will do will actually be done. And if it isn't done, the guilt will remind you of your failure. Guilt and blame are the psychological responses to broken promises, and require a memory of past sins. If we don't know our past, we can't feel guilt and act morally.

We are onto something intensely fundamental here, and therefore perhaps something difficult to comprehend. We are so accustomed to thinking that 'who we are' is essentially determined by the inner self or a set of fixed personality traits. Instead, if my thinking here is valid, 'who we are' is determined by our promises and obligations to others. Living up to our obligations is not just a chore, but a manifestation of what is important in life – and, basically, of who you are. In this context, dwelling on the past is essential. But it is also a process that is necessarily hazy. Our past – both personal and cultural – isn't a ready-made story that you can take in all at once. We are inextricably woven into events and relationships in ways that mean we don't always understand them. However, it is nonetheless crucial (especially on moral grounds) to draw links between our past, present and future, and not merely be content with being 'fully present in the moment'. This is also why the (auto)biography so poorly encapsulates a person's life. As we saw in the previous step, it is far too linear and individualistic a genre to portray real life in all its dazzling complexity. Dwelling on the past provides insights into the complexity of your life and how it is intertwined with all sorts of social and historical processes.

What can I do?

If you are now convinced of the value of dwelling on the past, there are two things you can do. One is to seek out existing communities that are determined by the past. It is difficult for an individual to do something that goes against the *zeitgeist*, so it may prove helpful to seek out like-minded individuals. If you can't find any, you'll have to do the work yourself – but more of that anon.

Just as individuals only understand themselves via knowledge of their own past – and how this past is interwoven with a wealth of relationships and obligations – so too is a community shaped by what it (or at least its members) knows about its past. This doesn't mean that a family or an association must be in complete agreement on what characterises it as a community or its history (they rarely will be). But there has to be some sort of minimal consensus among members. The philosopher Alasdair MacIntyre has developed a concept of 'living traditions', which suggests that traditions are entirely distinct from consensus and a simple repetition of the past. He defines a living tradition as 'an historically extended, socially embodied argument, and an argument precisely in part about the goods which constitute that tradition'.[6] It may seem strange to define a tradition as an 'argument' extended over time, but it suggests that any tradition – e.g. of political co-operation, educational practices or artistic activity – must involve a continuous discussion of what it is and how to legitimise or change it. Traditions aren't monolithic and unchanging (apart from dead ones, of course). They are living, dynamic and in constant motion.

It is when we participate in such traditions – in family life, education, work, art, sports etc. – that we become people. We only understand ourselves when we know the traditions from which we stem and within which we live our lives. This is quite banal, but we often overlook it in our enthusiasm for the future: without traditions and their history, nothing is meaningful. Any meaning and significance that an action or a cultural product may have draws on historically developed practices. You must therefore dwell on the past to understand yourself as a cultural and historical being or entity. Only then will you find something on which to stand firm.

According to the Stoic Seneca, those who are excessively busy do not contemplate the past: 'The engrossed, therefore, are concerned with present time alone, and it is so brief that it cannot be grasped, and even this is filched away from them, distracted as they are among many things', he wrote. If you want to be everywhere at once, you can't stand firm anywhere. Seneca says: 'The mind that is untroubled and tranquil has the power to roam into all the parts of its life; but the minds of the engrossed, just as if weighted by a yoke, cannot turn and look behind. And so their life vanishes into an abyss.' The good thing about the past, he claims, is that 'all the days of past time will appear when you bid them, they will suffer you to behold them and keep them at your will – a thing which those who are engrossed have no time to do'.[7]

It is therefore important to dwell on your own past, but also on the past of the culture in which you are embedded. And it would be even better if you were to practise living traditions. If, for example, you learn a craft or play an instrument, you will understand that this is only possible because the specific practice has a long history, which you help to maintain and develop whenever you recreate aspects of it. To practise living traditions is to be reminded of the historical depth of our lives. In this way, you learn that everything doesn't necessarily always move forwards. For example, it isn't possible to build violins today that are as good as the instruments built in Stradivarius' workshop more than 300 years ago. Not only are we not able to make such exquisite instruments nowadays, but we also find it difficult to produce *any* kind of object that might last that long – and even get better as time goes by. Our focus on the future is short-sighted, often limited to our own lifetime. If you are ever lucky enough to hold a Stradivarius in your hand, think of the virtuoso instrument-maker who built it and the many talented musicians who have played it over the centuries. Granted: I am resorting here to the worst kind of banal conservatism, but it's hard not to, when comparing such craftsmanship with the mass-produced flotsam and jetsam of today.

If you aren't lucky enough to have access to living traditions of this type and communities with a passion for art or music, there is still something you can do. As I wrote in the preamble to this chapter, practise repeating yourself. Look for role models who have put down roots. Insist on the right to stand still. It can be quite entertaining, when in conversation with enthusiastic acquaintances who focus on the future, to insist that everything was better in the old days. Of course, this isn't entirely correct, but it may serve as a useful corrective to the opposite dogma: that something is necessarily good because it's new. Or that we can simply 'download' whatever we need in the moment, without any appreciation of the past. There is great value in repetition and tradition, and innovation poses serious problems. However, at the risk of muddying the waters, I would add that, in a deeper sense, all repetition is innovative. I often repeat myself, e.g. when I teach or give lectures. But every talk is a unique event, with its own unique air to it. And if you are a parent with two children, you don't react to the arrival of the third child by saying 'Oh well, another one'. In a sense, we repeat ourselves when we have children. But each repetition (or child) is unique, needs just as much care and attention, and requires that we respond appropriately to its specific, individual needs. Parenting is a living tradition. Good parents (your own perhaps?) can serve as existential role models who are firmly 'rooted'. It's difficult to imagine anything more important than a binding relationship with individuals (children) for whom you have responsibility. When it comes to responsibility towards other people, stability is more important than mobility.

Some final thoughts

Once you have worked your way through the seven steps in this book, you will be better placed to withstand the manic development imperative so prevalent in contemporary culture. You have now been exposed to a wide range of concepts that explain aspects of our culture that make so many of us feel a vague sense of unease and discomfort. Hopefully, you are now able to distance yourself critically from 'the accelerating culture', with its foot ever harder on the pedal, and in which the ideal person is unconnected and relatively devoid of duties and commitments. In other words, somebody who has prioritised mobility over stability. More than ever, this individual is responsible for their own destiny and success in life. Strong individuals are the ideal. People who know themselves, place themselves (and the concept of the self) front and centre, know how they feel inside, and deploy their personal and emotional skills, both in the workplace and in private life – including their love life – to achieve their goals. They're left to find their own direction in life – and to quantify success in that endeavour in their own way – because all answers come from within. This is precisely why there is a thriving market for therapy, coaching and counselling designed to make you better at introspection, positivity and self-realisation. A whole series of self-development technologies have been institutionalised in various social arenas, including in performance and development reviews and personal development courses – not to mention the whole self-help industry.

Hopefully, reading this book has provided you with not only a language with which to understand these trends and verbalise your discomfort, but also techniques to help you stand firm rather than join in the eternal pursuit of self-development. You have learned the value of spending less time on introversion, focusing more on the negative, wearing your No hat, suppressing your feelings, sacking your coach (and other self-development gurus), replacing self-help literature with novels, and dwelling on the past rather than the future. I am well aware that I have painted a pretty negative picture in my attempt to counteract the trend towards coercive development. In fact, my alternative view risks being distorted just as easily as the positive celebration of the self, inner emotional life, authenticity, the Yes hat and self-development. My hope is that presenting a counterpoint in this way will illuminate the absurdity of the accelerating culture and its prevailing wisdom. It *is* absurd to be eternally mobile, positive and focused on the future, and to put the self at the centre of everything in life. Not only is it absurd, it also has adverse consequences for interpersonal relationships, as other people are quickly reduced to instruments to be used in the individual's pursuit of success, rather than an end

Dwell on the past

in themselves, to whom we have moral obligations. But I freely admit that it would also be absurd if we were *always* negative, always donned the No hat and suppressed our feelings.

In essence, my point of view is quite pragmatic – it is that nothing is always 100 per cent good. Apart from general, self-evident and quite abstract ideas (e.g. about doing your duty[8]), there is probably no such thing as absolute truth when it comes to ethical ideas or philosophies of life. This is the very essence of pragmatism: ideas are tools developed to solve life's problems. If the problems change, the intellectual tools used to solve them must change as well.[9] One of the starting points for this book is that the problems associated with life *have* changed in the past half-century. The basic problem used to be that life was overly rigid – stability was lauded over mobility. Now, it is overly flexible. In Step Four, I discussed the difference between the *prohibition culture* of the past (in which culture's morality revolved around a set of rules you must *not* break) and contemporary *command culture* (in which the basic ethos of the day calls for development, adaptation and flexibility). Previously, our problem was *wanting* too much. Now it is that we will never be able to *do* enough in a society that constantly demands we do more and more and more.

Economists and environmentalists regularly discuss whether there are 'limits to growth'. Well, the same applies to human and psychological issues. Is there a limit to how much growth and development is good for people? My answer, of course, is yes. The book's negativism – its antithetical relationship to everything related to development and positivity – is, in my opinion,

115

justified in an era of omnipresent and unbridled growth philosophy. What I hope to achieve with this book, above all else, is to hammer home that doubt is a legitimate and necessary virtue in our modern society. Doubt about whether the self can and should be the focal point of life. Doubt about whether (self-)development is good *per se*. Doubt about whether the prevailing ideology is good for people.

Of course, if we accept that doubt is indeed a virtue, then it must be applied to the recommendations made in this book as well. My main doubt about the book is whether this negativist alternative actually tacitly accepts the individualist premise it purports to contest. Isn't there a risk of adding to the burdens already heaped on the shoulders of individuals by exhorting them also to take these seven steps? It's a legitimate concern, but my hope is that by inverting the logic of the self-development mania, the book will highlight its absurdity. It's a fairly safe bet that positive or negative thinking alone won't solve the big problems the planet faces. Nevertheless, I do think that Stoic reflection acts as a refreshing tonic when confronted by runaway consumerism and coercive development. However, to use a medical analogy, this is just addressing the symptoms. Other types of discussion and action (political, economic, etc.) are needed if we are to cure the major ailments of the day (e.g. global environmental and economic crises) and the growth paradigm associated with them. I hope that this book has been useful to you as a very small part of that bigger discussion.

Appendix: Stoicism

The book frequently refers to Roman Stoicism. In several instances, I have highlighted what I believe are prime examples of clear Stoic thinking by Marcus Aurelius, Epictetus and Seneca. At this point, I hope that you will understand that my relationship with Stoicism (however much I admire these particular philosophers) is ultimately pragmatic. In other words, I don't think it's fruitful to ask if Stoicism is *true* in an absolute sense – at all times and in all places – but I do think we should consider whether it is *helpful* in the light of the problems we face in our day and age. As an 'anti-self-help philosophy' I definitely think it's useful, partly because it emphasises self-control, a sense of duty, integrity, dignity, peace of mind and a willingness to come to terms with (rather than find) yourself. It is also useful because several of the Stoics were concerned with how to make their philosophy part of people's everyday lives, e.g. via the techniques mentioned, including negative visualisation (the idea of losing what you have) and projective visualisation (gaining a sense of perspective by imagining your experiences happening to others). The Stoics were big on reason and believed that the deepest joy in life will be achieved by facing inevitability head on and with an unflinching eye – in particular, facing the fact that life is finite and that we *will* all die.

Fundamentally, human beings are vulnerable, not strong, self-reliant individuals. We are born helpless children, we often fall ill, grow old and perhaps helpless, and eventually we all die. These are the basic realities of life. However, much of Western philosophy and ethics has been based on the idea of the strong, autonomous individual, at the expense of our fragility and vulnerability, which have been all but forgotten.[1] Stoicism takes its starting point in the notion of *memento mori*, coupled with a social disposition and sense of duty. For while we are vulnerable and mortal, we are these things *together*. This realisation should rouse our sense of solidarity and encourage us to care for our fellow humans. Basically, the hope is that this book's seven-step guide will help you to do your duty. Fundamentally, life shouldn't be about trivial pursuits or adolescent identity crises (although these may be appropriate in certain stages of life), but about doing your duty. Stoicism is useful because, more than any other philosophy I know, *practical* implementation is very much at its core. The book may have whetted your appetite and left you wishing you knew more about the thinking behind Stoicism, so I will conclude with a brief introduction to the main Stoics and their ideas.

Greek Stoicism

Roman Stoicism may be better known, and it is the form referred to in this book, but Stoicism was born in

Appendix: Stoicism

Ancient Greece, as just one of many competing schools of philosophy. These schools related, in various ways, to the basic systems devised by Plato and Aristotle, and refined many of the ideas advocated by the two founding fathers of philosophy, turning them into practical philosophies of life. The first Stoic is thought to have been Zeno of Citium (333–261 BCE). He made his way to Athens from Cyprus after a shipwreck, and happened to meet Crates of Thebes, part of the Cynical school. At that time, Cynicism had a completely different meaning than it does today. In Greece, the Cynics were preoccupied with liberating themselves from dependence on the material world, with all its luxury and status symbols. They wandered the land in a self-imposed state of poverty and asceticism. The most famous of the Cynics is Diogenes of Sinope, who famously lived in a barrel, absolutely oblivious to normal conventions and ambitions.[2]

Zeno was a pupil of Crates, but became more and more interested in theoretical ideas rather than the Cynics' pretty extreme ascetic practices. He shaped the original form of Stoicism as a practical *and* theoretical philosophy. The word *stoicism* comes from the Greek word for portico, *stoikos*, as the Stoics met and taught at a place in Athens, called *Stoa poikile*, meaning 'Painted Porch'. Stoicism is therefore named after a part of the city of Athens. It arose out of the Cynics' asceticism, but also adapted it. Zeno – and later Stoics – didn't renounce the good things in life, they just pointed out the value of being prepared to lose them one day. The idea was that there's nothing wrong with good food and a comfortable home *per se*, as long as you don't become dependent on them. Zeno also linked practical

Appendix: Stoicism

philosophy, including ethics, with more theoretical and scientific disciplines, such as logic and physics (which in those days was more akin to cosmology). This underlines Stoicism's concern with humans as rational beings; in other words, as beings who have drives and instincts, but are capable of acting rationally, i.e. playing down their urges and training their instincts, whenever it is wise to do so. And doing so is often wise in pursuit of the good life. A good life is the ultimate purpose of Zeno's Stoicism (as well as the later Stoics). However, the term 'the good life' had a completely different meaning back then. Today, the concept is usually associated with a form of hedonism, a philosophy of desires, a life of positive, exciting and varied experiences. For the Greek Stoics, the good life – *eudaimonia* in Greek – was far more about living a *virtuous* life, in accordance with ethics. It is by living life in this way that people flourish, in the true sense, and realise their humanity.

For the Stoics, 'virtue' didn't relate to sexual mores (as it does nowadays when people bandy about archaic terms like 'a virtuous woman'). Rather, the virtues consisted of the characteristics that enabled people to live in harmony with their own nature. In this way, the concept of virtue can be applied to all living creatures – and, essentially, to everything that has a function. The knife's virtue is that it cuts. A knife that cuts well is a good knife. The heart's virtue is that it pumps blood around the body. A heart that pumps well is a good heart. Similarly, you are a good human if you do what is in your nature. But what is that? Here, the Stoics followed Plato and Aristotle, and determined that the function of humankind is to use our reason. Their thinking was based on the belief that no other living creature

Appendix: Stoicism

possesses anything like human reason. We are capable of thinking and speaking, reasoning logically and drawing up principles (laws) for social intercourse. This puts distance between us and our biological urges, and to some extent suppresses them. As far as we know, no other animal is capable of that – indeed, not all humans are equally capable of it either. However, through practising the virtues, you master your urges and may even become a Stoic sage and serve as an example to others. The Stoics see the ability to apply reason as the factor that makes it possible to do your duty, as you more clearly identify the morally correct course of action in any given situation. You aren't blinded by egotistical emotions or instincts. Reason is thus both theoretical (e.g. as used in disciplines like logic or astronomy) and practical (i.e. oriented towards the good life, both individually and collectively). Human beings are rational animals (*zoon politikon*, as Aristotle termed it) – in other words, social beings capable of building a rational social order, especially via legislation.

When Zeno died, Cleanthes of Assos (331–232 BCE) became the leader of the Stoic school. He was in turn replaced by the better-known Chrysippus of Soli (282–206 BCE), who did much to make Stoicism a popular philosophy of life. After his death, Stoic thought also reached Rome (around 140 BCE), when Panaetius of Rhodes (185–110 BCE) founded Roman Stoicism and became friends with well-known Roman figures such as Scipio Africanus the Younger (one of the most famous military commanders in history, who vanquished, among others, Hannibal). It is a unique feature of Stoicism as a philosophy that it found so much favour among the upper echelons of society. This is particularly true, of course, when it comes to Marcus Aurelius, the famous Roman philosopher-emperor. When Stoicism came to Rome, the Greek emphasis was on the importance of virtue, while peace of mind was of secondary concern. The Roman Stoics were also preoccupied with virtue and calls for people to do their duty, but they considered peace of mind a prerequisite for this. You can't do your duty without peace of mind, and as such it was seen as a stepping stone on the road to virtue.

Part of the transition from Greek to Roman Stoicism was the decline in interest in logic and physics. The Greek Stoics thought of the world as a cohesive unit – a cosmos. In philosophical terms, they were monists, i.e. they believed that everything is basically composed of the same substance. This also applies to their psychology (i.e. when considering the nature of the soul). Here, Stoicism is in line with modern science, which has abandoned the idea that there are essentially different substances in the world (e.g. soul vs body), although Stoic thinking on this was occasionally ambiguous. On the other hand, modern science – by which I mean the scientific worldview that began to emerge with the likes of Galileo in the early seventeenth century and later on with Newton – presents other challenges to Stoicism. Not least in terms of the Stoic insistence that human beings have a purpose derived from human nature itself. Modern, mechanical natural science rejects the Greek idea of purpose, meaning and value in nature. Instead, nature is seen as a mechanical system that functions according to certain principles of cause and effect, as formulated in the laws of nature. As Galileo famously put it, 'the Book of Nature is written in the language of mathematics'. To the extent that there *is* purpose, meaning and value, they are purely psychological projections onto a nature that, in itself, is devoid of such characteristics. Without being able to go into this more deeply in the current context, this is where we find the natural-science breakthrough that – to quote sociologist Max Weber's famous phrase – 'disenchants the world' while 're-enchanting' the human mind. It is here that we, in our era of modernity, should seek the essential aspects of life, i.e. ethics and values. However, there is also a price to pay – these aspects are subjective and lean towards the psychological, which leads to the idea of the importance of what is inside you and the religion of the self, as I have called it in this book. When the 'outer world', as a purely mechanical system, is unable to provide answers to life's big questions, we have to sanctify the 'inner world'.[3]

Stoicism affords us an opportunity to 're-enchant' the world (and not just the mysterious 'inner world'), and as such obviates the need to frantically search within ourselves for answers. Of course, we can't just copy a cosmology developed 2,500 years ago in Ancient Greece. We need to work on our own understanding of how the 'exterior' points the way forwards for human beings. The central message of this book – which, in this sense, is in line with Stoicism – is that by looking at the traditions, social practices and relationships of which we form a part, and the duties arising from them, we might regain the ability to address questions about the meaning and value of life. However, this requires that we forego our desperate preoccupation with the internal and self-development, and instead learn to connect in more appropriate and meaningful ways to the pre-existing relationships in our lives. By reflecting in

Appendix: Stoicism

this way, we might be able to fulfil our duties, live more virtuous lives (in the Stoic sense) with greater peace of mind, and even feel a sense of reassurance that it all makes sense.

But back to the story of Stoicism, and what happened when it arrived in Rome.

Roman Stoicism

Most philosophers and historians of ideas consider Seneca, Epictetus and Marcus Aurelius to be the key Roman Stoics. Seneca is perhaps the best writer among them. He was born about 4 BCE in Cordoba, Spain, and became a highly successful businessman in Rome, where he also served as senator. His wealth may help explain his appointment as advisor to Emperor Nero. In 41 CE, after political intrigue of a type not uncommon in those days, he was exiled to Corsica and stripped of his riches due to a (probably false) accusation of a sexual relationship with a niece of the then emperor (Claudius). In Corsica, Seneca had time to immerse himself in philosophy and develop his Stoic thinking. After eight years, he was pardoned and returned to Rome, where he became Nero's teacher and, later, advisor. Seneca committed suicide in 65 CE on Nero's order (because Nero thought Seneca was conspiring against him). Aside from that of Socrates, Seneca's death is probably the most mysterious in the history of philosophy. It is said that he first slashed his wrists and then drank poison, but failed to die. Eventually, his friends took him into the steam room, where he suffocated and finally did shuffle off his mortal coil.

Seneca's writings – which I have quoted several

times in this book – are exceptionally practical and to the point. They mostly consist of letters to friends and acquaintances, providing advice and instructions about how to live their lives – and they always take into account the brevity of life. If a modern reader were to ask Seneca how to get the most out of this short life, the answer would not be to experience as much as possible, but to live a serene life with peace of mind and your negative emotions under control. Seneca's writings reflect an approach to humanity reminiscent of the one preached, almost contemporaneously, by Jesus of Nazareth. It is therefore no surprise that his thoughts have often been compared with the tenets of Christianity (albeit without the latter's metaphysical aspects). For example, Seneca wrote, 'To avoid anger with individuals, you must forgive the whole group, you must pardon the human race.'[4]

Epictetus was born a slave around 55 CE. He was owned by the emperor's secretary, and was therefore probably exposed to the intellectual life at court. Following Nero's death, he was granted his freedom, a not entirely uncommon occurrence among educated, intelligent slaves. He left Rome and founded his own school of philosophy in Nicopolis in western Greece. Irvine says that Epictetus wanted his students to feel bad when they left the school – as if they had visited the doctor and been given bad news.[5] Being introduced to Stoic thinking and learning to reflect on life's brevity was no picnic! Like Seneca, Epictetus too was extremely practical in his writings on the philosophy of life. He described all kinds of situations – from insults to incompetent slaves – and issued advice on how to tackle them. As with the other Stoics, he advocated living with peace of mind and dignity, even in times of adversity. This could be achieved by striving to live a life based on reason, the essential element of human nature. For example, Epictetus applied reason to distinguishing between that which it is possible to control and that which it is not. In essence, you should prepare for the uncontrollable (e.g. the weather, economic fluctuations, your own mortality), but it's a waste of time to worry about it or fear it. You should train yourself to take an active approach to the things you can do something about (e.g. becoming a more generous human being). All that it takes to distinguish one from the other is a dose of reason.

Marcus Aurelius (121–80 CE) is known as the philosopher-emperor. Since his childhood, he had been interested in philosophy and intellectual affairs. He retained these interests in adulthood, and often spent time thinking and writing, even during campaigns in remote parts of the Roman Empire. Marcus was one of the most humane emperors in the history of Rome – perhaps the best of them all. Unlike most other emperors, he wasn't interested in personal gain, and took a parsimonious approach to politics, e.g. to finance wars, he preferred to sell off imperial possessions rather than raise taxes. The Roman historian Cassius Dio wrote that Marcus remained unchanged from his earliest days in politics (when he was an advisor to Antoninus Pius until the death of the latter). In other words, he stood firm on his integrity and consistently navigated through life on the basis of his ideas of good and evil. He died in 180 CE after an illness, and both the citizens and soldiers of Rome mourned his death. However, his life and death did not lead to any great surge in interest in Stoicism, as he largely kept his philosophy of life to himself. His most famous work, *Mediations*, is also called 'To Himself' and was only published after his death.

Another Roman deserves to be mentioned, although he is not a Stoic in the strict sense. Cicero (106–43 BCE) is unavoidable in Latin literature and thought. He was a politician, and was involved in the violent events surrounding the death of Julius Caesar. His subsequent opposition to Marcus Antonius (aka Mark Antony) cost him his life. In his letters and other texts, Cicero refers to the Stoics as 'allies', and quotes Socrates' statement that philosophy is an exercise in dying well. Cicero's main themes are the good life and the good death, but he was also concerned with the public good. His masterpiece is perhaps *De Officiis* (On Duties), in which he asks – based on Aristotle's conception of man as a rational political animal – what duties are specifically associated with being human. If you would like to gain an insight into some of the best political writing in history, I recommend *On Living and Dying Well* – a collection of letters and speeches in which Cicero address themes including fear of death, friendship and duties.[6]

In modern times, one of the most insightful analyses of Stoicism as a practical philosophy was written by the historian of philosophy Pierre Hadot. He sought to summarise the main ideas of Stoicism in its many different forms, and ultimately arrived at four key points: (1) the Stoic consciousness of the fact that no being is alone – we are all a part of a larger whole (the cosmos); (2) all evil is moral evil, and therefore pure moral consciousness is important; (3) the belief in the absolute value of the human person (out of which originates the idea of human rights); and (4) a focus on the present moment (living as if we were seeing the world for the first and last time).[7] Hadot's four points also help explain the selective application of Stoicism in this book. In many ways, the first three points encapsulate the book's view of humanity – with a focus on humans as relational and moral beings with intrinsic value. On the other hand, I have not used, but rather indirectly criticised, Stoicism's emphasis on the importance of the moment. I don't believe that humankind mainly lives in the moment, but in time as an extensive and continuous structure. This focus on the present, and on the individual's power to determine how they will be affected by what is happening right *now*, closely resembles the current self-development wave ('you can choose to be happy *now*!'). In my view, this gives the individual too great a responsibility for how he or she meets the world. I don't believe that we can freely choose how we will be affected by the present. To the extent that this is a Stoic ideal, I would say that Stoicism should be challenged on this central point. We are, to a far greater extent than the Stoics would accept, impotent – indeed, the realisation of this can act as a source of solidarity between people.

While this book does not mount an uncritical defence of Stoic philosophy, I believe that – for those who find the coercive development wave, with its rudderless mania of development for its own sake, discomfiting – it is uplifting to discover that, more than 2,000 years ago, thinkers had already developed a fruitful and thoughtful philosophy that teaches you how to stand firm. Simply being aware of this and similar traditions will better prepare you for life in the accelerating culture. You will derive comfort from the fact that there is an alternative

Appendix: Stoicism

to the pursuit of eternal positivity, self-development and authenticity – an alternative which stresses that the finest things about human beings are our sense of duty, peace of mind and dignity. I believe that much of the Stoic humanist view should be resurrected in the twenty-first century, now that we have a need, more than ever, to learn to stand firm – together.

Notes

Introduction

1 This metaphor was introduced by the sociologist Zygmunt Bauman. See his book *Liquid Modernity* (Polity, 2000) and numerous later works that analyse love, fear, culture and life itself in the light of the 'liquidity' concept.

2 I analysed this in the article 'Identity as Self-interpretation', *Theory & Psychology*, 18 (2008), pp. 405–23.

3 This is demonstrated by the sociologist Hartmut Rosa in the books *Alienation and Acceleration: Towards a Critical Theory of Late-Modern Temporality* (NSU Press, 2010) and *Social Acceleration: A New Theory of Modernity* (Columbia University Press, 2015).

4 Anders Petersen has described this many times, e.g. in the article 'Authentic Self-realization and Depression', *International Sociology*, 26 (2011), pp. 5–24.

5 Anthony Giddens introduced the concept of the pure relationship, e.g. in *Modernity and Self-identity: Self and Society in the Late Modern Age* (Routledge, 1996).

6 This theme is addressed in depth in *Det diagnosticerede liv – sygdom uden grænser* (The Diagnosed Life: Illness Without Borders), which I edited (Klim, 2010).

7 See Zygmunt Bauman's *Liquid Times: Living in an Age of Uncertainty* (Polity Press, 2007), p. 84.
8 See their book *The Wellness Syndrome* (Polity Press, 2015).
9 For an accessible introduction that stresses the practical side of Stoicism, see William B. Irvine's *A Guide to the Good Life: The Ancient Art of Stoic Joy* (Oxford University Press, 2009).

Chapter 1: Cut out the navel gazing

1 http://www.telegraph.co.uk/finance/businessclub/management-advice/10874799/Gut-feeling-still-king-in-business-decisions.html
2 http://www.femina.dk/sundhed/selvudvikling/5-trin-til-finde-din-mavefornemmelse
3 See Philip Cushman's article 'Why the Self is Empty', *American Psychologist*, 45 (1990), pp. 599–611.
4 Søren Kierkegaard, *Either/Or*, Part II (Gyldendals Book Club, 1995), p. 173.
5 Analysed by Dr Arthur Barsky in the article 'The Paradox of Health', *New England Journal of Medicine*, 318 (1988), pp. 414–18.
6 See http://www.information.dk/498463
7 Honneth posits this in several works, including the article 'Organized Self-realization', *European Journal of Social Theory*, 7 (2004), pp. 463–78.
8 For an analysis of this trend, see Luc Boltanski and Eve Chiapello, *The New Spirit of Capitalism* (Verso, 2005).
9 Richard Sennett has demonstrated this in several books. Best known is *The Corrosion of Character: The Personal Consequences of Work in the New Capitalism* (W. W. Norton & Company, 1998). The paradox-generating nature of late capitalism is analysed by Martin Hartmann and Axel Honneth in the article 'Paradoxes of Capitalism', *Constellations*, 13 (2006), pp. 41–58.

10 Jean-Jacques Rousseau, *Confessions* (1782).
11 Irvine, *A Guide to the Good Life*, see especially chapter 7.

Chapter 2: Focus on the negative in your life

1 E.g. in the article 'The Tyranny of the Positive Attitude in America: Observation and Speculation', *Journal of Clinical Psychology*, 58 (2002), pp. 965–92.
2 This has been noticed – and criticised – e.g. by Barbara Ehrenreich in the book *Bright-sided: How the Relentless Promotion of Positive Thinking has Undermined America* (Metropolitan Books, 2009).
3 See his interesting post at http://www.madinamerica.com/ 2013/12/10-ways-mental-health-professionals-increase-misery-suffering-people
4 I dealt with positive psychology in far greater detail in the chapter 'Den positive psykologis filosofi: Historik og kritik' (The Philosophy of Positive Psychology: History and Criticism) in the book *Positiv psykologi – en introduktion til videnskaben om velvære og optimale processer* (Positive Psychology: An Introduction to the Science of Well-being and Optimal Processes), edited by Simon Nørby and Anders Myszak (Hans Reitzels, 2008). Seligman's most famous book is *Authentic Happiness* (2002).
5 See Rasmus Willig, *Kritikkens U-vending* (The U-turn of Critique) (Hans Reitzels, 2013).
6 The article in *Berlingske Tidende* is available online (in Danish) at: http://www.b.dk/personlig-udvikling/positiv-psykologi-er-ikke-altid-lykken
7 Translated from http://www.lederweb.dk/Personale/Med arbejdersamtaler-MUS/Artikel/79932/Vardsattende-med arbejderudviklingssamtaler
8 Barbara Held, *Stop Smiling, Start Kvetching* (St Martin's Griffin, 2001).
9 The quotation is translated from Irene Oestrich's self-help book *Bedre selvværd: 10 trin til at styrke din indre*

GPS (Better Self-esteem: 10 Steps to Strengthen your Inner GPS) (Politiken, 2013), p. 193.

10 See Irvine, *A Guide to the Good Life*, p. 69.
11 Seneca, *Livsfilosofi* (selection of Seneca's moral letters by Mogens Hindsberger) (Gyldendal, 1980), p. 64.
12 This is discussed by Oliver Burkeman in *The Antidote: Happiness for People Who Can't Stand Positive Thinking* (Canongate, 2012).
13 Quoted from Simon Critchley, *How to Stop Living and Start Worrying* (Polity Press, 2010), p. 52.

Chapter 3: Put on your No hat

1 Per Schultz Jorgensen, *Styrk dit barns karakter – et forsvar for børn, barndom og karakterdannelse* (Strengthen Your Child's Character: A Defence of Children, Childhood and Character Formation), (Kristeligt Dagblads Forlag, 2014), p. 75.
2 http://www.toddhenry.com/living/learning-to-say-yes
3 Anders Fogh Jensen, *Projektsamfundet* (The Project Society) (Aarhus University Press, 2009).
4 Critchley, *How to Stop Living and Start Worrying*, p. 34.
5 Nils Christie, *Small Words for Big Questions* (Mindspace 2012), p. 45. Thanks to Allan Holmgren for drawing this fine little book to my attention.
6 For example, in the book *Contingency, Irony and Solidarity* (Cambridge University Press, 1989).
7 Hannah Arendt, *The Human Condition* (University of Chicago Press, 1998), p. 279.

Chapter 4: Suppress your feelings

1 This is a major theme in Søren Kierkegaard's writings. For example, in *The Sickness Unto Death*, the self is defined as a relationship that relates to itself. Along with the Norwegian psychologist Ole Jacob Madsen, I

described the psychology built into the story of Genesis in the article 'Lost in Paradise: Paradise Hotel and the Showcase of Shamelessness', *Cultural Studies ↔ Critical Methodologies*, 12 (2012), pp. 459–67.

2 A good source is his book *Liquid Times: Living in an Age of Uncertainty.*

3 http://coach.dk/indlaeg-om-coaching-og-personlig-udvikling/lever-du-et-passioneret-liv/350

4 Her book on the subject is called *Cold Intimacies: The Making of Emotional Capitalism* (Polity Press, 2007).

5 Arlie Russell Hochschild described this emotional work in *The Managed Heart: Commercialization of Human Feeling* (University of California Press, 1983).

6 Richard Sennett, *The Fall of Public Man* (Penguin, 2003, originally 1977).

7 E. Harburg et al., 'Expressive/Suppressive Anger Coping Responses, Gender, and Types of Mortality: A 17-Year Follow-Up', *Psychosomatic Medicine*, 65 (2003), pp. 588–97.

8 C. H. Sommers and S. Satel, *One Nation Under Therapy: How the Helping Culture is Eroding Self-Reliance* (St Martin's Press, 2005), p. 7.

9 See R. Baumeister et al., 'Does High Self-esteem Cause Better Performance, Interpersonal Success, Happiness, or Healthier Lifestyles?', *Psychological Science in the Public Interest*, 4 (2003), pp. 1–44.

10 This research is discussed in Barbara Held's *Stop Smiling, Start Kvetching.*

11 Seneca, *Om vrede, om mildhed, om sindsro* (On Anger, On Gentleness, On Peace of Mind) (Gyldendal, 1975).

12 The example is mentioned in Irvine, *A Guide to the Good Life*, p. 79.

Chapter 5: Sack your coach

1 This analysis is based on my article 'Coachificeringen af tilværelsen' (The Coachification of Life), *Dansk Pædagogisk Tidsskrift*, 3 (2009), pp. 4–11.

2 Religious sociologists have long used terms such as 'the sacralised self' to identify the sanctification of the self in contemporary practices such as therapy, coaching and New Age thinking. See, e.g., Jacob Ole Madsen, *Det er innover vi må gå* (And inwards we must go), (Universitetsforlaget, 2014), p. 101.

3 This was one of the main themes in Kirsten Marie Bovbjerg's insightful studies of working life, e.g. 'Selvrealisering i arbejdslivet' (Self-realisation at Work) in Svend Brinkmann and Cecilie Eriksen (eds), *Self-realisation: Critical Discussions of a Limitless Development Culture* (Klim, 2005).

4 See the article in *Berlingske Nyhedsmagasin*, 31 (October 2007).

5 See Willig, *Kritikkens U-vending*.

6 I know that positive psychology also recommends what is called 'random kindness', a kind of spontaneous charity. However, here the motivation is for the giver to feel good inside. I would argue for the intrinsic value of the benevolent act, irrespective of any emotional impact on the person responsible for it. You should do good deeds because they are good. Not because they make you feel good – although it is no bad thing if the deed makes you feel good as well.

Chapter 6: Read a novel – not a self-help book or biography

1 Charles Taylor, *The Ethics of Authenticity* (Harvard University Press, 1991), p. 15.

2 I should point out that only some biographies fall into this category. Not all biographies are linear or trivial. Indeed, I am a relatively avid reader of (auto)biographies.

But they work best when they ignore the conventions of the genre.

3 Ole Jacob Madsen, *Optimizing the Self: Social Representations of Self-help* (Routledge, 2015).

4 See Thomas H. Nielsen, 'En uendelig række af spejle – litteraturen og det meningsfulde liv' (An Infinite Number of Mirrors: Literature and the Meaningful Life), in C. Eriksen (ed.), *Det meningsfulde liv* (The Meaningful Life) (Aarhus Universitetsforlag, 2003).

5 See Jan Kjærstad's article 'Når virkeligheden skifter form' (When Reality Changes Shape), *Information* (30 September 2011).

6 See Foucault's posthumous *Technologies of the Self* (Tavistock, 1988).

7 See also 'On the Genealogy of Ethics: An Overview of Work in Progress', in P. Rabinow (ed.) *The Foucault Reader* (Penguin, 1984).

8 This reading of Houellebecq builds on an earlier analysis published in the article 'Literature as Qualitative Inquiry: The Novelist as Researcher', *Qualitative Inquiry*, 15 (2009), pp. 1376–94.

9 Michel Houellebecq, *Atomised* (Vintage, 2001), p. 252.

10 Hubert Dreyfus and Sean Kelly, *All Things Shining: Reading the Western Classics to Find Meaning in a Secular Age* (Free Press, 2011).

11 Oscar Wilde, *The Complete Works* (Magpie, 1993), p. 32.

Chapter 7: Dwell on the past

1 http://www.ankerhus.dk/teori_u.html

2 Critchley, *How to Stop Living and Start Worrying*, p. 118.

3 See, e.g., Thomas Thaulov Raab and Peter Lund Madsen's popular science work *A Book About Memory* (FADL's Publishing, 2013), which champions this basic point of view.

4 In Denmark, these perspectives are best propounded by my colleague Professor Lene Tanggaard.

5 Paul Ricoeur, *Oneself as Another* (University of Chicago Press, 1992), p. 158.

6 The quotation is from his book *Whose Justice? Which Rationality?* (University of Notre Dame Press, 1988), p. 12.

7 All the quotes here are from Seneca, *On the Shortness of Life* (Vindrose, 1996), p. 30.

8 In this book, I have regularly used the phrase 'doing your duty', but without really defining the concept. This is because I believe that duty is always concrete, not abstract. People have duties by virtue of their specific relationships to other people. You have a duty to your mother, father, manager, employee, teacher, student, etc. K. E. Løgstrup pointed out in his book *Den etiske fordring* (The Ethical Demand) that you must use your power over others for their good, not your own. The phrase 'ethical demand' is close to the concept of duty used in this book – and is both as open and as concrete. See *Den etiske fordring* (Gyldendal, 1991, original 1956).

9 In my opinion, the most interesting pragmatist philosopher is John Dewey, about whom I have written a number of articles and books, including *John Dewey: Science for a Changing World* (Transaction Publishers, 2013).

Appendix: Stoicism

1 This is one of the main themes in Alasdair MacIntyre's *Dependent Rational Animals: Why Human Beings Need the Virtues* (Carus Publishing Company, 1999), in which he places our existence as vulnerable animals at the centre of a virtue-based system of ethics.

2 My historical review of philosophy is based in particular on Irvine's *A Guide to the Good Life.*

3 This story is told best by Charles Taylor in his *Sources of the Self: The Making of the Modern Identity* (Cambridge University Press, 1989).
4 Seneca, *Om vrede, om mildhed, om sindsro*, p. 27.
5 Irvine, *A Guide to the Good Life*, p. 52.
6 Cicero, *On Living and Dying Well* (Penguin Classics, 2012).
7 Pierre Hadot, *Philosophy as a Way of Life* (Blackwell, 1995), p. 34.